PASSPORT
VIETNAM

I HOPE THIS IS
THE FIRST OF MANY!

Passport to the World

Passport Argentina
Passport Brazil
Passport China
Passport France
Passport Germany
Passport Hong Kong
Passport India
Passport Israel
Passport Italy
Passport Japan
Passport Korea
Passport Mexico
Passport Malaysia
Passport Philippines
Passport Russia
Passport Singapore
Passport South Africa
Passport Spain
Passport Taiwan
Passport Thailand
Passport United Kingdom
Passport USA

PASSPORT VIETNAM

Your Pocket Guide to Vietnamese Business, Customs & Etiquette

Jeffrey E. Curry
"Jim" Chinh T. Nguyen

Passport Series Editor: Barbara Szerlip

WORLD TRADE PRESS®
Professional Books for International Trade

World Trade Press
1505 Fifth Avenue
San Rafael, California 94901 USA
Tel: (415) 454-9934
Fax: (415) 453-7980
USA Order Line: (800) 833-8586
E-mail: WorldPress@aol.com

"Passport to the World" concept: Edward Hinkelman
Cover and book design: Peter Jones
Illustrations: Tom Watson
Cover photography: Global Directions, Inc., San Francisco

THIS PUBLICATION IS DESIGNED TO PROVIDE GENERAL
INFORMATION CONCERNING THE CULTURAL ASPECTS OF
DOING BUSINESS WITH PEOPLE FROM A PARTICULAR COUN-
TRY. IT IS SOLD WITH THE UNDERSTANDING THAT THE PUB-
LISHER IS NOT ENGAGED IN RENDERING LEGAL OR ANY
OTHER PROFESSIONAL SERVICES. IF LEGAL ADVICE OR OTHER
EXPERT ASSISTANCE IS REQUIRED, THE SERVICES OF A COM-
PETENT PROFESSIONAL PERSON SHOULD BE SOUGHT.

Library of Congress Cataloging-in-Publication Data
Curry, Jeffrey E. 1953 - / Nguyen, Jim Chinh T. 1967 -
Passport Vietnam: your pocket guide to Vietnamese business, customs
& etiquette / Jeffrey E. Curry & Jim Chinh T. Nguyen
p. cm. -- ("Passport to the world")
Includes bibliographical references (p.).
ISBN 1-885073-25-9
1. Corporate culture -- Vietnam. 2. Business etiquette -- Vietnam. 3.
Industrial management -- Social aspects -- Vietnam. 4. Negotiation in
business -- Vietnam. 5. Intercultural communication. I. Title. II. Series.
HD58.7.T485 1996
390'.009597--dc20
96-14867
CIP

Printed in the United States of America

Table of Contents
Vietnam

The Ascending Dragon

Overview

1: Doing Business Across Cultures 6
   Vietnam Quick Look 8
2: Country Facts 9
3: The Vietnamese 12
4: Cultural Stereotypes 23
5: Regional Differences 26

Business Environment

6: Government and Business 29
7: The Work Environment 36
8: Women in Business 40
9: Making Connections 42
10: Strategies for Success 45
11: Time 49
12: Business Meetings 51
13: Negotiating with the Vietnamese 58
14: Business Outside the Law 65

Customs & Etiquette

15: Names & Greetings 70
16: Communication Styles 74
17: Customs 78
18: Dress & Appearance 81
19: Reading the Vietnamese 83
20: Entertaining 85
21: Socializing 89

Additional Information

22: Basic Vietnamese Phrases 92
23: Correspondence 93
24: Useful Numbers 94
25: Books & Internet Addresses 95

1 Doing Business Across Cultures

Although business operations around the world have become highly standardized, national traditions, attitudes and beliefs remain diverse. Public praise, for example, is much enjoyed by its recipient in the U.S. and Europe, but it's a source of embarrassment and discomfort for Asians. This is because Western cultures value individual thought and action, while Eastern cultures prize modesty and consensus.

While the primary focus of people in one culture might be to quickly get down to business, another culture concentrates on first developing personal relationships. Although their objectives may be the same, people from different cultures are likely to have different ways of achieving them.

You'll probably never know a particular culture as well as your own — not only is the language different, but the historical context within which its people operate is often misunderstood by outsiders.

Passport Vietnam will offer some insights into the country and its inhabitants and help you understand how their traditions, values, business practices and communication styles differ from your own.

Comparing Values Across Cultures	
One Culture:	**Another Culture:**
Values change	Values tradition
Favors specific communication	Favors ambiguous communication
Values analytical, linear problem solving	Values intuitive, lateral problem solving
Places emphasis on individual performance	Places emphasis on group performance
Considers verbal communication most important	Considers context & nonverbal communication most important
Focuses on task and product	Focuses on relationship and process
Places emphasis on promoting differing views	Places emphasis on harmony and consensus
Emphasizes competition	Emphasizes collaboration
Prefers informal tone	Prefers formal tone
Is flexible about schedules	Emphasizes rigid adherence to schedules

Vietnam
Quick Look

Official name   Socialist Republic of Vietnam
Land area   329,707 sq km
Highest Elevation   Mt. Fan Si Pan 3,143 m
Capital   Hanoi
Largest City   Ho Chi Minh City (HCMC)
People
  Population   73 million
  Density   215 per sq km
  Distribution (1995)   23% urban, 77% rural
  Annual growth (1995)   2.2 percent
Official language   Vietnamese
Major religions   Buddhism, Catholicism,
                           Taoism

Economy (1995 est)
  GDP   US$25 billion
                           US$325 per capita
  Foreign trade   Imports — US$2 billion
                           Exports — US$2 billion
  Principal trade partners China/Taiwan/Hong Kong
                           Japan
                           Singapore
                           Eastern Europe
  Currency   1 dong = 100 xu
  Exchange Rate (7/96)   10,991 dong = US$1
Education and health
  Literacy (1995 est)   88 percent
  Higher Education Insts 104
  Hospital beds (1991)   208,400
  Physicians (1989)   1 for every 3,140 people
  Life expectancy (1995) Women — 66 years
                           Men — 62 years
  Infant mortality (1995) 51 per 1,000 live births

VIETNAM

Country Facts

Geography and Demographics

Vietnam lies between China and Cambodia and is bordered by the Gulf of Thailand, the Gulf of Tonkin and the South China Sea. Its terrain varies from low, flat delta to central highlands to mountains, and it's home to one of the world's great rivers, the Mekong (known as *Song Cuu Long*, "River of the Nine Dragons"). The rich Mekong Delta covers 23,000 sq. miles and produces much of Vietnam's food.

The populace is comprised primarily of ethnic Vietnamese (*Kinh*) and Chinese. More than half are in their teens and early twenties, having been born after the end of the Vietnam War. The *Khmer, Thai, Man, Cham, Meo, Hmong, Muong* and some 46 other "colorful" ethnic minorities are considered potential tourist attractions by the government.

Climate

The weather is basically tropical, but considerably cooler in the mountainous interior highland areas. In the north, temperatures range from 16°C / 60°F in the winter (a.k.a. the dry season, November through April) to 30°C / 85°F in the summer (a.k.a. the wet season, May through October). Winter is a dry, dusty period in the Hanoi area.

In the south, the temperatures are fairly constant year-round (25° to 30°C / 76° to 85°F). Rain storms are sudden and torrential. Typhoons are fairly common in coastal areas between July and November.

Business Hours

Most businesspeople arrive at their offices between 8 – 8:30 A.M. Monday through Saturday and remain until 4:30 P.M. Banks are open Monday through Friday from 8 A.M. until 4 P.M., with a break between 11:30 A.M. and 1 P.M. (Many Vietnamese nap during the hottest part of the day, often on the cool floor tiles of their office or on straw mats.) They close at 3 P.M. on Saturdays and 11 A.M. on the last working day of each month. Government offices are open from 7:30 A.M. to 4:30 P.M. Monday through Friday and until 11:30 Saturday mornings. Posted office hours are not always reliable, so it's always wise to call ahead.

Larger retail shops generally follow the same hours as offices, though it's becoming more common to find stores open well into the evening, especially in Ho Chi Minh City. Smaller shops, street vendors and many of the restaurants frequented by locals open as early as 4:30 A.M. (The Vietnamese have a relaxed attitude toward schedules, but they're willing to accommodate themselves to a customer's needs.)

National Holidays

New Year's Day .... January 1

Tet (Traditional .... (varies) 1st to 7th day of new
    New Year)   lunar year, late Jan./early Feb.

Hai Ba Trung Day .... Honors the Trung Sisters, who
                             fought the Chinese in A.D. 40 —
                             (varies) 6th day of 2nd lunar
                             month

Liberation of South .... April 20
    Vietnam and Saigon

Thanh Minh .... Family shrines are cleaned and
    (New Year of   decorated. 3rd lunar month,
    the Dead)   usually April 5th or 6th

Int'l Labor Day .... May 1

Anniversary of Birth ... May 19
    of Ho Chi Minh

Buddha's Birthday ...... Pagodas and temples are deco-
                             rated with lanterns. May 28

Trung Nguyen . . . . It's believed that prayers can
    (Wandering   absolve the sins of the dead,
    Souls Day)   who leave Hell for a day to
                             return home. (varies) 15th day of
                             7th lunar month

National Day .... September 2

Trung Thu .... Based on legend about a king
    (Mid-Autumn   who encountered an incredibly
    Festival)   beautiful spirit in Heaven.
                             Special cakes are baked and
                             children walk through towns
                             holding lanterns. (varies) 15th
                             day of 8th lunar month

Confucius' Birthday .... (varies) 28th day of 9th lunar
                             month

(For more on holidays and festivals, see Customs:
Chapter 17).

The Vietnamese

Mythic & Historic Past

The Mountain Princess *Au Co* and the Dragon Lord *Lac Long Quan* are the mythological parents of the Vietnamese race. Beautiful Ha Long Bay (Descending Dragon) recalls in its jagged islands how extraordinary creatures helped shape the land. Virtually every city has a street that commemorates the battle of Dien Bien Phu and the expulsion of the French. Statues of war heroes, ancient and contemporary, can be found in even the smaller towns. Everywhere, Vietnam honors the patriots, battles and complex myths of its past.

A recurrent theme in the country's history has been the arrival, absorption and expulsion of foreign invaders, colonizers and interlopers. Although the southern section of Vietnam was wrested from the ancient Cham civilization, the Vietnamese see themselves as the rightful rulers of a land that was hand-picked for them by the gods. It is both their duty and their destiny to protect that country for future generations.

For over a thousand years beginning in 111 B.C.E., China ruled over Vietnam, dominating every aspect of society. For hundreds of years during that period,

Vietnamese mandarins were sent to be trained in Chinese cities. Though finally expelled in the mid-10th century, the Chinese continued to exert great cultural influence. It wasn't until the French arrived in the 1850s that Vietnam ceased to use Chinese-style characters for writing.

The French plundered the small country for its resources, both human and commercial. Control was absolute and maintained with a brutality that still reverberates today. (Hundreds of Vietnamese died in Hoa Lo prison — the famous "Hanoi Hilton" — long before it was used as a prison for American pilots. It's currently being turned into a commercial complex, but its original French colonial walls are being left as a reminder of past sufferings.)

During World War II, the Japanese took over from the defeated French. Only recently have the stories been documented of the over one million Vietnamese killed by starvation during this period, as the Japanese shipped Vietnam's rice crops back home to feed their own countrymen. It was also during this period that Ho Chi Minh (aka: *Nguyen Tat Thanh* and *Nguyen Ai Quoc*) rose to power. After World War II, the United States gave him the choice of having either the French or Chinese return as de facto rulers. Ho Chi Minh's reply to the American liaison, though unprintable here, implied that he thought he would have an easier time expelling the French than the Chinese.

Thomas Jefferson & "The American War"

The French were, in fact, defeated in 1954 at the battle of Dien Bien Phu, and a century of domination came to an end. This one battle is so pivotal in Vietnamese history that it's re-enacted on a daily basis at the war museum in Hanoi. After the French withdrew, the country was to be temporarily divided (pending elections) at the 17th parallel along the border between Quang Tri and Quang Binh provinces. Many anti-communists, Catholics and intellectuals fled to the south to escape repression by the newly formed northern regime.

Fearing the "domino effect" — that Southeast Asian countries would fall to the communists one by one — the United States had been supplying Vietnam with military advisors for some time. Then, in 1965, the U.S. sent the first in a series of "official" combat troops to support the newly designated Republic of Vietnam, south of the dividing line. Over the next ten years, over ten million troops and support personnel flooded in, from the U.S. and elsewhere. (What was called the Vietnam War was known locally as "The American War.") Russia and China came to the aid of their political brethren in the north.

Though a committed communist, Ho Chi Minh had based his 1945 revolutionary constitution on Thomas Jefferson's *Declaration of Independence* (the line "All men are created equal" appears in both documents) and had repeatedly attempted to enlist U.S. support for an independent, nonaligned Vietnam. Now, he set his sights on "liberating" the South from external influence and uniting the country under communist rule at all costs. The resulting clash wore down the American political resolve; war footage and weekly body counts broadcast on American TV helped to spur a nationwide anti-war movement. After a long drawn-out peace process, accords were signed in Paris in 1973. The South, left to its own defenses, fell to North Vietnam's forces two years later.

A New Republic

In 1976, after twenty years of brutal warfare that resulted in over 3 million Vietnamese deaths, the nation was formally reunited under the title of Socialist Republic of Vietnam. The vacuum created by the U.S.'s abrupt departure resulted in Vietnam's incursion into Cambodia in 1978. This, in turn, resulted in a brief but costly border war with China in 1979. Vietnam was victorious in both instances. It was also during this post-war period that the massive exodus of political and economic refugees (known as "The Boatpeople") transpired. Hundreds of thousands of Vietnamese fled their homeland and scattered across the globe. Unknown numbers perished in the effort. Many were placed in "transit" camps in the countries where their seacraft landed and remain there today, still fighting against repatriation.

With the collapse of the Soviet Union's economy in the 1980s, Vietnam found itself without its largest benefactor (and most recent interloper). Desperate, the central government decided to throw aside its strict adherence to communist doctrine and embrace a policy of market economics. (See Doi Moi, page 30.)

Many political and economic observers have remarked on this seeming triumph of free markets over centrally planned economies. But the larger truth is that this recent course change is part of a longterm pattern. Historically, the Vietnamese have pursued whatever course was deemed necessary to preserve their culture for future generations.

Language

Tieng Viet is a source of great national pride. Monosyllabic, tonal and given to regional dialect, it's a distinctive indicator of class, education and sometimes even political affiliations. Word meanings vary, depending on inflection. (*Ma*, with various diacritic marks, can mean anything from rice seedling, horse or grave to mother or ghost.) Nearly half of the lan-

guage's vocabulary has Chinese origins; much of its
modern form is the result of a conscious effort by
subsequent generations to distinguish the *Viet* culture from that of its former oppressors. *Tieng Viet*'s
roman-style alphabet was devised in the 17th century by Catholic missionaries.

Vietnam's recent preoccupation with free markets and international commerce has caused a major
upsurge in the interest to learn English. English is *the*
language to learn if one desires advancement within
government or private industry. Fluency in English
is more likely to be found in the south.

Nationalism: Nobody's Lapdog

The Vietnamese are resolute nationalists. Their
strong sense of community has been partly attrib-
uted to their 4000-year dependence on rice cultiva-
tion, which requires cooperation on a large scale. It
also stems from having withstood — and eventually defeated — Chinese emperors and French colo-
nials, as well as 20th century Japanese and
Americans. There's also a strong, traditional attach-
ment to one's ancestors, and therefore to the physical land in which they're buried.

Although exceedingly poor by international
standards and in dire need of financial assistance,
Vietnam maintains a cautious attitude toward foreign investment. Foreign partners must aggres-
sively court the Vietnamese even to get a foot in the
door, and the government has made it exceedingly
difficult for foreign companies to bring in expatriates to run their operations. The country embraces
an "investment, not investors" policy. Vietnam, as
the Chinese say, "is nobody's lapdog." And they
should know.

The Family

It is to the family that the Vietnamese owe their strongest allegiances. Most of the population lives in extended family units (often consisting of several generations) in which each member contributes something to the overall well-being of the group. The education of children is a priority (though sons are favored), and poverty is not considered an excuse for ignorance.

The Western sense of "private space" is not a Vietnamese concept. While many are poor, even well-to-do families live in close proximity to each other (sleeping in the same room, for example) by choice. There's a sense of communication, trust and a pleasure in human contact.

Family connections are a key part of the culture; their importance should never be underestimated. They're particularly tight in business and government, where nepotism is expected and encouraged. The paucity of Vietnamese family names reflects the strength and extent of such connections.

However, it's also true that pervasive influences from the West, coupled with a disproportionately young population (half under the age of twenty-one), are undermining the strength of such family ties.

How the Vietnamese View Themselves

Vietnam has a primarily Buddhist culture. Lighting incense at a family shrine is as integral to contemporary life as watching videos, riding a motorbike, or listening to the BBC or *Voice of America* on the radio.

Suffering is accepted as an inescapable part of human existence. Adversity is faced with pragmatism, patience and calm and people tend to look to the long-term when solving problems. The group takes precedence over the individual; solutions must satisfy the consensus. The Vietnamese have very little regard for those who lose patience or exhibit selfishness.

The Vietnamese are proud, but judiciously so. And like many newly independent nations, they're suspicious of outsiders and demonstrate a readiness to exploit foreign weakness to their advantage.

Viet Kieu

Viet Kieu, the general term for overseas Vietnamese, is most often applied to those who left the country after 1975. France is home to Europe's largest *Viet Kieu* population, and some 900,000 reside in the U.S.

Officially, the government welcomes *Viet Kieu* and encourage their participation in the country's development, even going so far as to decree preferential tax treatment for *Viet Kieu* investors. It hopes that the infusion of hard currency and technical skills into the economy will duplicate the effects felt in China by the influx of overseas Chinese.

In practice, however, Vietnamese authorities still harbor a distrust of the overseas Vietnamese community. Unlike China's expatriates, many of whom left for economic reasons, most of Vietnam's former residents left for political ones. They are often questioned thoroughly and intrusively by customs and immigration authorities when traveling in and out of the country, and extortion at transit points is not uncommon.

There are indications that native Vietnamese also dislike and distrust their overseas brethren, whom, they believe, abandoned their homeland. The *Viet Kieu* interpret that distrust as envy. (But the situation isn't without occasional humor. In Ho Chi Minh City, a bar opened by sixteen Vietnamese-

Americans offers *Viet Kieu* cocktails — ingredients unknown.)

Many Western businesspeople are eager to team up with a *Viet Kieu* as a shortcut to overcoming both language and cultural barriers. In some cases, however, such collaboration can be risky or even detrimental. Some ministry officials have explicitly stated that having a *Viet Kieu* as the principal in a foreign enterprise will expose the project to delay, or even prevent approvals. Some *Viet Kieu* have gone so far as to seek Westerners to act as "team leaders" while projects are in their formative stages.

Some of this problem stems from resentment of the *Viet Kieu* and some from a bias that favors Westerners. The Vietnamese tend to defer to Westerners when discussing technology, markets, higher education or finance. But this deference appears to be waning.

Most Vietnamese, especially the police, can instantly spot a *Viet Kieu*. Even though they have made an effort to bring presents to their Vietnamese relatives, the *Viet Kieu* will be put upon to "share" their wealth. Those visiting from the United States are deemed to be especially wealthy and must be prepared for solicitations from all quarters.

Some *Viet Kieu* have an understandable ambivalence about returning to a country that doesn't always welcome them. Others are eager to return and move the country into a richer future. In both cases, the pull of the homeland is strong and can summed up in the proverb:

We ought to return and bathe in our own pond,
Whether the water is muddy or clear.

Attitudes Toward Foreigners

The Vietnamese are sincere in their desire to extend hospitality and to learn about what life is like in other countries. Foreigners are often struck by their friendliness. Invitations to visit people's home for meals or to join in family events are not uncommon.

At the same time, the Vietnamese often see foreigners as "money," and they're somewhat distrustful of them (businesspeople, in particular). And as they've demonstrated over hundreds of years, they can be fearsome enemies when threatened. Many are interested in the benefits of "modernization" while remaining averse to anything that will bring with it the environmental problems of Thailand or the economic chaos of the Philippines. But how much development is too much? Where should the line be drawn between tradition and progress?

The West isn't viewed as a monolith. Vietnamese can easily spot the difference between an American and a German or between a Frenchman and a British subject. It's as easy for them as distinguishing a Chinese from a Japanese. Westerners are seen as being particularly skilled in business, and the United States as preeminent. U.S.-made products are revered, and the U.S. is thought of as an economic and military buffer between them and their Asian-Pacific neighbors. (The Vietnamese word for "America" is the same as the word for "beautiful".)

France serves as Vietnam's European link, and its influence is quite manifest — from high literacy and world class culinary skills to aging French colonial buildings that lend an elegance to many Vietnamese cities.

China's impact is millennia old, deeply ingrained and often resented. The Vietnamese have not forgotten China's past repression of them, and they continue to distrust the Chinese who have made Vietnam their home. While Vietnam may fear economic colonialism from the West and Japan, physical occupation by the Chinese is still recognized as a very real possibility.

Cambodia is a traditional enemy with some shared heritage. Much like the Viet-Sino relationship, Vietnam casts a wary eye across the Cambodian border (where skirmishes still erupt), while maintaining strong political influence over its other close neighbor, Laos. Vietnam's recent acceptance as a member of ASEAN (Association of Southeast Asian Nations) also points to a policy of controlling its future via association rather than isolation.

Social Evils

Within the country's Communist Party, there are those who believe that Westerners are set on undermining Vietnam's heritage, morals and economy by means of "peaceful evolution" — that is, via capitalism and consumer goods. As of February 1996, the government began stepping up enforcement against such "social evils" as sexy calendars and magazines (publicly burned), tens of thousands of overly violent or "black" (pornographic) video tapes (crushed under steamrollers), and foreign name-brand billboards such as Pepsi, Coca Cola, Panasonic, Kodak, Fuji and Heineken (ripped down, painted over or covered with tape). Hundreds of karaoke bars (which sometimes front for brothels) have been raided, closed, or severely restricted to ensure that no pre-1975 Saigon music (now officially banned) is played. Citizens are being asked to sign pledges that they won't watch the aforementioned videos (which are believed to inspire lives of crime), gamble or fraternize with prostitutes. As in China, Vietnam's Communist Party is struggling to retain control as the economy opens up. (Party membership is estimated at 2.2 million, out of a total population of 73 million.) In-country observers insist that this is a passing phase.

On another front, some Vietnamese newspapers have expressed concern about the possibility of foreign companies using Vietnam as a dumping ground for their obsolete technologies.

How Others View the Vietnamese

Nearly all would agree that the Vietnamese are enterprising and industrious. Their hands are never idle, and if something can be made from nothing, the Vietnamese are the people to do it.

Centuries of conflict, ideological wars, an economy ravaged by central planning and recent embargoes left the Vietnamese with little but an indomitable spirit by the latter half of the 20th century. They were miles behind the "Asian dragons" with no means to catch up. Their biggest benefactor, Russia, failed them and they languished near the bottom of the world's economies. The government struggled and the people made do.

Motorbikes and other machines were repaired until workers were re-welding the welds. Over 70 million people were kept fed by an agricultural system structured for far fewer. These traits did not escape the world's notice, and despite the U.S.'s embargo set on severing all trade, other nations soon saw the value in trading with these industrious people.

For many Westerners, however, impressions of the Vietnamese obtained during the Vietnam War, and Hollywood's subsequent depiction of that conflict, are the most vivid and ingrained. Vietnam's most recent isolation, during the post-1975 embargo period, only served to reinforce those impressions. While it's true that the Vietnamese are fierce and aggressive fighters with no small potential for brutality, these same attributes can be used to describe a variety of cultures — from both the First and the Third World.

4 Cultural Stereotypes

Stereotypes about Vietnam abound. Some are based on personal experience, some on knowledge gained from others, and some from historical stereotypes and prejudice built on hearsay. These perceptions will color and influence the way you approach your business relationships with the Vietnamese. To the extent that they are realistic assessments, they will probably help you. Those that are outdated or inaccurate will hinder your ability to get along.

Aggressive

The Vietnamese are aggressive and brutally repressive of dissent.

This impression is born of 20th century conflicts with France and the U.S., as well as Vietnam's military incursion into Cambodia (which seemed to confirm beliefs that the Vietnamese were pursuing an expansionist war policy).

However, since its withdrawal from Cambodia, followed by a brief conflict with China, Vietnam has remained at relative peace. Recent skirmishes in the South China Sea over the Spratley Islands will most likely be resolved around an ASEAN negotiating table. Vietnam learned from its victory over the U.S. that "winning" a war can be a very mixed blessing. Their energies have now been turned toward conquering market economics and the enemy of poverty.

The Vietnamese see themselves as woefully behind many of their Asian neighbors, and foreign businesspeople should be warned not to mistake an eagerness to succeed with naked aggression.

Visitors should also keep in mind that political dissent isn't tolerated. Even Buddhist monks are regularly imprisoned for taking an anti-government stance. "Re-education" camps are a very real aspect of Vietnamese politics.

Duplicitous

The Vietnamese are duplicitous and cannot be trusted, especially in business.

In many Asian cultures, directness is not a valued trait. Most Vietnamese will readily admit that what is openly expressed in gestures and words is far from "the whole truth," and that they often have ulterior motives or hidden agendas — especially when dealing with foreigners. And they assume that foreigners are playing the same game (though perhaps to a lesser degree).

However, they don't view such behavior as duplicitous or deceitful. Rather, it's part of the politeness and consideration so valued in their culture. Directness and complete honesty can lead to conflict — and conflict, particularly in public, must be avoided at all costs.

Obsessed with Work

The Vietnamese are workaholics.

Even the casual visitor to Vietnam will see a population working around the clock in both the countryside and the cities. (And in other parts of the world, the *Viet Kieu* have earned a reputation for overcoming adversity with their tenacious labor.)

But many Western and Asian businesses sing a different song about their employees in Vietnam — often complaining that they're undisciplined, unmotivated and unproductive. The terms "lazy" and "shiftless" have been used more than once. Some foreign operators have even been prosecuted for beating their employees in an attempt to raise productivity.

Foreign companies must realize that they are entering a market formerly devoted to communism and central planning. One of the oldest adages of the communist worker is "We pretend to work and you pretend to pay us." Many Vietnamese, especially in the north, have never known any other system.

Foreigners are perceived to be wealthy capital- ists with bottomless pockets. For the Vietnamese, the concepts of profit and productivity are very new, and most of them, even managers, have had positions guaranteed by the state. Being terminated for poor performance was virtually unknown.

The professionalization of middle-manage- ment and supervisory personnel will go a long way toward changing the situation. The recent establish- ment of Vietnamese management schools points in the direction of a solution in the near future.

Productivity is just one of many areas in which Vietnam must play "catch-up." Foreign businesses must make sure that their training programs extend beyond the technical aspects of the job. Like any- where else, an employee's ability and willingness to work hard depends on their motivation.

5 Regional Differences

A Continuing Rivalry

For centuries, northerners worked within close proximity to the ruling powers and were told what to do and when. Whereas in the south, there was less supervision and people learned to make their own decisions. This history (along with other factors) has led to two different ways of getting things done. North Vietnam remains traditional and rigid in its approach, while South Vietnam can be characterized as assertive, lively and innovative.

The long-term rivalry between these regions was dramatically shaken in 1975. After the Vietnam/American War, many northerners were sent south to govern their defeated relatives. The ensuing resentment, augmented by property confiscations and re-education camps, continues into the present day. Ironically, with an increase in the importance of the market economy, Southerners are now busy swallowing up the bulk of foreign investment and have taken on an "I told you so" attitude.

The North (Ha Noi)

Hanoi (literally, "city on a bend in the river") is

Vietnam's capital and official political center. It's a city of tree-lined boulevards, weathered French colonial villas, elegant squares, and the occasional defunct bomb shelter. Despite the rush to modernize, there's now a major push to preserve what remains of the city's thousand-year-old Ancient Quarter (with its narrow, winding streets named for the craftspeople who once lived there — Basket Street, Gold Street, Fan Street, Shoe Street) and the French Section. After a colonnaded arcade near *Hoan Kiem* lake (where, according to myth, a king found a sacred sword on the back of a giant turtle) was torn down by high-rise developers, officials began to reconsider the city's redevelopment plan.

The hope is to avoid turning Hanoi into another Bangkok, Singapore or Shanghai — shiny new Asian cities without distinction or character. While the government's motive is partly financial (i.e. tourist appeal), it's also partly based on genuine sentiment. Meanwhile, a strong lobby is pushing for fast, unfettered growth.

The South (Thanh Pho Ho Chi Minh)

Ho Chi Minh City (HCMC), the industrial, business and cultural heart of Vietnam, was once known by the name of its central district: *Saigon*. A cosmopolitan city of Asian traditions and Western influences, it's distinguished from Hanoi by a tremendous growth rate and a free-wheeling entrepreneurial spirit. (One communist leader recently described HCMC as a "hotbed" for "hostile forces" seeking to subvert party rule.) Every product and service imaginable, in every price range, can be found here. Though home to only seven percent of the population, it's responsible for 20 percent of the country's GDP, 33 percent of industrial output and the bulk of foreign trade and investment.

Vietnam's economic reforms are most evident here, and annual household incomes are estimated to be at least twice as high as in the North. HCMC is home to the *Cho Lon* district which, by virtue of having Vietnam's highest concentration of ethnic Chinese, is credited with having maintained much of the free market activity prior to 1986.

The city, which is being almost entirely rebuilt, boasts the closest thing to Vietnamese "skyline." Buses, cars, bicycles, motorcycles, pedestrians and sometimes even oxcarts all share roads built for half their present number. Traffic has become so bad that the traditional but cumbersome cyclos (pedicabs) have been banned in some districts.

The Countryside

Countryside dwellers identify with either the north or south but couple those loyalties with rural values. Visitors are welcomed warmly, but efforts to undertake business are met with indifference or intense haggling with provincial officials anxious to receive a piece of the action. Most rural inhabitants manage to eke out a living from either the land or the sea; incomes are sometimes less than 10 percent of the urban average.

Indeed, it's this huge majority of the population that acts as a brake on economic development. Transportation, water treatment, power and communication infrastructures are minimal and, in some cases, nonexistent. Consumer goods are scarce but on the rise. The central government's recent concern over this area focuses on keeping the population from flooding into the cities — in search of jobs and a slice of the free-market good life.

6 Government and Business

Although the government has loosened its economic grip and, to some extent, its social one, Vietnam remains a one-party communist state. Besides regulating businesses, the government also owns and runs many of them. It's virtually impossible to conduct business without the support, and often the participation, of the government or military.

The government does, however, seem to recognize the value of a relatively hands-off approach, if only to attract foreign investment. Vietnam is by no means the most attractive venue for those wishing to invest in Asia. (Even Myanmar, formerly Burma, has more liberal investment policies and regularly permits 100 percent foreign-owned enterprises with lucrative profit-repatriation packages.) But Vietnam does have over 70 million potential consumers — half of them under the age of twenty-five. The country is particularly in need of companies that can expand and upgrade its roads, bridges, ports, airports and railroads.

There's an active domestic and foreign financial press, but they freely admit to government censorship. Good news is highly touted; bad news is reported weeks after the fact, if at all. The country's

commercial statistics were officially declared to be
state secrets in 1995. (Vietnam takes many of its
information handling cues from China.)

Although there have been continued complaints from foreign businesspeople about telephone taps and spying, evidence points to this
practice having declined in recent months. Still, the
government has made recent forays into Internet
and advertising control, and it remains interested
in the activities of foreigners — so be careful about
what you say and to whom you say it.

Doi Moi

For decades, private shops were banned, work
incentives were disallowed and international trade
was shunned. Then, in 1986, a new economic policy
was announced. Dubbed *doi moi* (literally "renova-
tion"), it called for the gradual abolition of the vast
bureaucratic system and state subsidies; businesses
were to become privately financed and self-sustain-
ing. It was, in short, a wholesale transformation —
from a centrally planned, socialist nonperformer
into a tumultuous, profit-driven "open door" system that encourages free enterprise and foreign
investment. Both reformers and hard-liners agreed
that *doi moi* was the only way to modernize the
country's economy. The speed and scope of the process were the only areas of contention.

Doi moi's major features included:

- Decollectivization of farming, resulting in far
  greater individual control over crops and profits
- Introduction and encouragement of private
  industry outside the state run sector
- Greater autonomy for state enterprises and individual regions (particularly in the south), with
  more discretion to respond to market conditions

- Dismantlement of price controls and reduction of state subsidies for many goods and services
- Encouragement of foreign investment and an active attempt to compete regionally for it

Soon after *doi moi* was introduced, Vietnam was targeted by carpetbaggers who saw the country as a kind of Wild West, but their quick-fix deals soon fell apart. Today, development can be seen (and heard) in the guise of pile drivers, bulldozers, hammers, drills and ever-worsening traffic jams. There are twice as many cars and four times as many motorbikes as there were in 1990 (and eight times as many telephones). Construction cranes hover over streets busy with BMWs and Mercedes-Benzes carrying business tycoons to their appointments. Five years ago, Hanoi had no taxis; now there are hundreds of them.

As of 1996, Vietnam is the world's third leading rice exporter. Investments totaling US$18 billion are on record, and a lot more are expected to follow. Even small investments flourish: in HCMC, locals can choose from among all thirty-one flavors of Baskin-Robbins' ice cream.

But while *doi moi* is reaping results, it's still not clear whether this will create more than just small pockets of wealth within an otherwise destitute, and increasingly dissatisfied populace. Reduced government aid has resulted in the deterioration of education and healthcare for the poor (more than half the nation). A free market system within a predictable, regulatory network has yet to be established. Banking remains primitive, and a stock exchange has yet to materialize. And while some Politburo officials are pushing for change, others view *doi moi* as a threat to both the fabric of Vietnamese society and the Communist Party's long-term power.

It's important to realize that though the government has loosened some of the reins of economic decisionmaking, it retains an authoritarian hold. Under the guise of reducing the number of state-controlled businesses, the government has consolidated many of its holdings — combining shoe, belt and other leather businesses, for example. And as is the case with political dissent, serious criticism of the economy isn't tolerated.

The Law on Foreign Investments

Originally formalized in 1990, Vietnam's Law on Foreign Investments is the government's single most important manifestation of *doi moi*. It's provisions encourage "foreign organizations and private persons to invest capital and technology ... in any sector of the economy" and guarantee that neither invested monies nor resulting assets will be expropriated, requisitioned or nationalized. But unfortunately, like many laws in Vietnam, this one is in a state of flux; seems to change on a quarterly basis and implementation is piecemeal. Businesspeople would be well advised to keep abreast.

Foreign investment experienced inconsistent growth for several years; the government acknowledges that 1996 will show a decrease. Some of this is attributable to tighter government policy and the fact that many investors have come to realize that Vietnam's potential is a long way from fruition and that profits will be hard won.

The Law on Foreign Investments promises some very real benefits for US$50 million-plus ventures and for projects promising technology transfers. Experienced negotiators have found that the law exhibits a flexibility proportional to the size of the investment package.

The SCCI / MPI

The State Committee for Cooperation and Investment (SCCI) has recently merged with the State Planning Committee to form the Ministry of Planning and Investment (MPI). In cooperation with other ministries and provincial authorities throughout the country, it devises, develops and regulates projects that require foreign investment. For foreign businesspeople hoping to break into the Vietnam market, the MPI is the place to start. (Such ministries and authorities as local Peoples' Committees also have the power to advance or cancel your project.)

Developing initial contacts with the MPI is vital not only to getting approved, but also to attaining the most favorable terms. The MPI may wish to discuss the amount of capital you're pledging, the value being prescribed to each business partner's nonliquid capital (such as land rights, machinery and technology transfers) and whether your project qualifies for reduced or deferred taxation.

The Chamber of Commerce and Industry of Vietnam (VCCI) can also lend assistance to foreign businesses seeking opportunities and contacts.

Obstacles to Consider

Even if you gain all the necessary approvals, basic infrastructural deficiencies can seriously impede your ability to conduct business efficiently and profitably. The highway system is poorly developed, and paved roads are scarce outside of major population centers. Some roads are impassable during the rainy season and the government is slow to repair damage. Overland transportation of goods is thus inherently unreliable, and at best, quite cumbersome.

Communication is another problem. Telephones are in short supply outside of the large cities, and even within them, connections are often bad. Fax services are expensive and e-mail is in its nascent stages.

Although direct dialing for international calls is available, rates are prohibitively high. Foreign businesspeople are sometimes reduced to communicating internationally by mail, which is relatively reliable but slow. Unless you represent a government agency, don't expect the Vietnamese to return overseas telephone calls or faxes. If, however, in your original correspondence you state a date and time when you'll call again, they will usually do their best to be available.

Power outages and voltage spikes are becoming a thing of the past in cities, but smaller towns and the countryside have inconsistent or inadequate power. Disruptions in business operations, communications, computers and air conditioning must be tolerated to varying degrees throughout the country.

One of the largest impediments to doing business in Vietnam is the overshadowing bureaucracy. Obtaining an investment license can sometimes require the approval of a dozen ministries or committees, and foreign businesspeople often find themselves sinking into a swamp of red tape. Although many top officials make serious efforts to streamline the process, their authority is limited and dispersed. The provinces still retain tremendous power, and this often manifests itself in the form of petty competitions. Provincial authorities will, in many instances, overturn or simply ignore permits and approvals obtained from the central government. (The central government is in the process of curbing some of this power.)

Seeking guidance from pioneer investors who entered the Vietnamese market years ago is well worth the time and money required. Tell them your plans and heed their advice; most are forthcoming with information. There is so much business potential and investment opportunity that business operators exhibit very little rivalry, except in the case of proprietary information. And their failures and successes are a much more dependable road map than the (often self-serving) advice you may receive from Vietnamese officials, who have been known to be confused about the legal and ministerial requirements of their own government.

Insiders and Outsiders

Vietnamese business is very strongly based on personal relationships. There's a definite advantage to being an insider — or having a connection to one. In fact, your success may depend on it.

You need not expend millions of dollars or be well known to be an insider. Due to the enormity of the country's commercial needs, small entrepreneurs have as much chance as the big guys — *if* they can develop and maintain the appropriate personal relationships.

The Vietnamese are very open to meeting people, but they will not conduct business with strangers. Socializing always precedes business dealing. Foreigners must make the effort to court ministers, mid-level clerks and local People's Committees. Take care with what you offer during meetings. While the Vietnamese don't observe contract law, they always hold foreigners to even the most casual promises made during meetings.

The government of Vietnam believes that it has already driven out the "cowboy" investors who swarmed over their country on the early 1990s. They have little patience with those who aren't interested in a long-term commitment.

7 The Work Environment

Vietnamese companies run the gamut — from family-run businesses operating out of the front room of a home, to street peddlers, to large, bureaucratic corporations with strictly defined functions. To date, there seems to be little in the way of common structure or method; the primary observation to be made is one of rapid change and lots of flexibility.

Capitalism and the quest for profits are relatively recent arrivals, and the Vietnamese have approached the new opportunities they've engendered with characteristic innovation and industriousness. The head of a successful manufacturing operation may have been a military commander a decade ago, while many university graduates drive taxis. In short, anything goes — and often does.

The business environment is literally changing day by day. If you're uncomfortable with unstable circumstances, Vietnam is not for you. The Vietnamese are unschooled in modern business practices, but they understand the necessity of adapting and they're eager to try new methods to gain higher profits.

Not The Only Game in Asia

The continued influx of non-Vietnamese businesspeople has drastically altered the face of the marketplace. In the early stages of *doi moi,* the government and business community took a "take it or leave it" attitude toward foreign investors. Joint ventures were always set up with the Vietnamese as the controlling partner, even if they had put up little or nothing in the way of capital or technology. Often, the nature of an agreement would change in accordance with the whims of local bureaucrats or in response to other, seemingly better, offers elsewhere, even after the "final" papers had been signed and the deal "closed."

Those times have passed. Today, investors can drive harder bargains, because the Vietnamese have come to realize that they're not the only game in Asia. Though far from perfect, Vietnam's business atmosphere is more favorable to serious investors than it's ever been.

Capitalists at Heart

The hardworking nature of the people doesn't always translate over into foreign-run operations. Long accustomed to over-staffed and underproductive state-run enterprises, many Vietnamese are finding it difficult to fit into streamlined, western-style organizations.

Especially in the manufacturing sector, employees are assigned to an enterprise by the local People's Committee and wage distribution is overseen by that same committee. And it's very difficult to discipline or terminate a Vietnamese employee because of the stringency of the labor laws. These two factors give the average worker little incentive to work above minimal capacity.

Luckily for foreign investors, labor is cheap and low productivity can be offset by an increase in the staffing. And productivity will most likely increase as capitalism becomes more entrenched and the economy speeds up.

Entrepreneur's Paradise

The Vietnamese seem to be entrepreneurs by nature. Every house that faces a business street seems to have turned its front room into a warehouse and storefront, complete with pull-up doors that reveal cartons and crates full of every product imaginable. "If a papaya falls from a tree," the Vietnamese say, "it's for sale before it hits the ground."

Even the slightest skill can be turned into profit, and those without skills act as middlemen. Major highways and every village road are lined with street stalls, where visitors who stop are routinely swarmed by children, teens, parents and grandparents selling everything from gasoline to T-shirts.

This bodes well for foreign investors. Many of the goods and services they offer will have a ready-made (though primitive) distribution system. Absolutely everything is needed in Vietnam — American and Japanese goods in particular. Brand loyalty is intense, most of the populace is young, and "salesmanship" is not considered to be a dirty word.

Competitive Socialism

Anyone who has gone to the race track in western Ho Chi Minh City can bear witness to Vietnamese competitiveness. Many locals are embracing a competitive commercial spirit. Although the government is careful to maintain an officially socialist regime, socialism as an economic policy exists in name only.

This is not to say that Vietnam has been given over to selfishness. On the contrary. Many of the current batch of entrepreneurs realize that the fruits of their labor are destined to benefit the next generation, rather than their own.

Decisions, Vietnamese-style

The Vietnamese follow the Asian system of decision by consensus, with a premium placed on harmony. Foreigners will almost never be aware of any dissension among his or her Vietnamese associates, and insider information will rarely be forthcoming from them. The system demands uniformity. Although Vietnamese are more open to forthright discussion than other Asians, they're still loathe to engage in confrontation (which is inconsistent with courtesy and harmony). With responsibility taken by the group, therefore, no one stands out above the rest. While this eliminates individual responsibility for failure, it also makes it more difficult for talented individuals to shine.

Several personal visits are often necessary before any overt signs of actual decision-making are seen — so don't be disappointed if decisions take much longer than you might expect. The Vietnamese rely on their personal relationships and the need to "save face." They will go out of their way to make something work if they think favorably of you; if not, your deal will probably not be accepted, regardless of how good it is.

It's important to be sure that you're dealing with the highest level of personnel available. While underlings have some impact and can exert considerable influence, it is the top echelon you will ultimately need to impress.

 ## Women in Business

Traditional Roles

Historically, women were expected to "pull their own weight." They often took on a significant amount of agricultural work, while shouldering most of the responsibility for raising their children. (Families of twelve or more were not uncommon.) At the same time, they were expected to defer to men in public.

Additionally, in a country plagued by war, the lack of males on the homefront often thrust women into positions in local government and service institutions (much of their work took place behind the scenes and went uncredited). Women also participated in combat (they're not required to serve). Military parades regularly feature "girl guerillas," and the national *Hai Ba Trung* Festival, celebrated in February, honors the memory of two sisters who led a rebellion against the Chinese.

Present Day Rights

Vietnamese women can vote (though with a one-party system, this may not be much of a benefit), and they have the right to hold property leases (though no one can technically own land under the communist system). While the culture holds education in high regard, (Vietnam's first national university predates England's Oxford University by 200 years), few females are educated beyond high school. When economics is a concern, families will educate male children at the expense of their daughters. Divorce is permissible; however, the rules for marital fidelity are quite lax for both sexes (though not publicly flaunted). Contraception isn't readily available.

It's noteworthy that because of Vietnam's nearly three decades of war, women over the age of twenty-five greatly outnumber the men in some provinces. Hundreds of thousands of them have had no choice but to remain single in a society that places enormous emphasis on marriage and childbearing.

Foreign Businesswomen in Vietnam

Vietnamese businessmen are most comfortable dealing with other men. However, foreign businesswomen should face few obstacles in pursuing their objectives.

A female team leader can make it abundantly clear that she is in charge by putting her name at the top of a team list and by emphasizing her credentials and accomplishments. She can ensure that the Vietnamese honor her status by instructing her team to 1) defer to her when questions are directed to others that would normally be put to her and 2) refrain from disagreeing or engaging in a "brainstorming" session in front of the Vietnamese.

Foreign businesswomen will probably be included in evening business activities — though there may be some discomfort on the part of Vietnamese males, who aren't accustomed to entertaining females in this capacity. Try to make it easier for them by going along with whatever is planned.

9 Making Connections

Relationships are Key

Personal connections are absolutely essential in Vietnam; put simply, you won't get anywhere without them. Generally, the Vietnamese will not even consider doing business with someone with whom they're not thoroughly acquainted. The business community is still small enough that many "players" know and routinely deal with each other and many are related by blood or marriage. This can work to a foreigner's advantage, however. The right connections will follow you throughout the country. (But so, too, will bad or mishandled ones.)

Some overly zealous Vietnamese have a habit of exaggerating the importance and usefulness of their "connections." Don't take their claims at face value.

Government agency and ministry connections will prove especially helpful, as they have final authority over most of the country's business transactions. As the rules are in a state of flux, ministry clerks may have authority far out of any proportion to their positions in the hierarchy.

Keep in mind that the Golden Rule applies. The better you treat your contacts, the better you'll be treated in return. Nurture them.

Introductions

The Vietnamese are very open to meeting foreigners with ideas or capital, and it's not difficult to
set up introductory meetings. People are willing to
share information and provide assistance to a
greater extent than in other developing Asian economies. This openness will lessen as competition
intensifies. But for now, it's easy to strike up a conversation almost anywhere, with anybody, and
even the most casual social encounter can result in
a business lead.

Your first trip to Vietnam should be of a research
nature. Spend some time observing and learning,
and "network" with as many people as possible —
key government and business leaders, citizens you
meet on the street, and foreign businesspeople who
are already somewhat established in Vietnam. Most
investment service companies and private consultants will agree to an introductory "information inter-
view" meeting. As elsewhere in the world, buying
someone lunch can prove to be the best investment
you'll ever make.

Finding a Good Partner

Having a local partner is just a fact of life in
Vietnam. Everyone except major international companies are required to have one. Choose your partners carefully — there are many more failures than
successes in this frontier economy.

Many people will claim to be intimately connected to the prime minister or other key official.
While this may be true, it's important to verify
such assertions. If the prospective partner can't
set up a meeting with their "contact" while you're
in the country, it's probably wise for you to look
elsewhere.

Although the Vietnamese are very eager to embrace capitalism and entrepreneurship, they are, for the most part, unskilled in how to do so. Many will make promises that they simply cannot keep. Since they will not bring many management skills or capital to the table (often, what they offer are land-use rights), you must be certain that their contacts are both viable and valuable.

Try to establish a trial period before committing to a long-term relationship. It's also essential to investigate a potential partner's financial and commercial status. The expatriate business community can be very useful in this regard. (You can be sure that *your* credentials will be verified by the Vietnamese.)

The MPI and the VCCI, as well as the local People's Committees, can also help you identify partners. Even when you receive a recommendation from these governmental sources, be sure to corroborate their information.

Businesspeople are also well-advised to nurture their relationship with the government. Name-dropping is very effective in Vietnam.

Yesterday's Fax = Today's Fish Wrap

Be aware that telephones and faxes are sometimes monitored by the government for security reasons. Copies of business correspondence have been known to find their way to ministries and even to the offices of other foreign companies — so be careful about revealing too much to potential partners early in the process. Some foreigners have reported stories of colleagues finding "confidential" faxes being used as wrapping paper in local stores. While such tales may be apocryphal, most expatriates living in Vietnam would find them to be within the realm of possibility.

 Strategies for Success

The Vietnamese Way

Many Westerners like to set a schedule or agenda and adhere to it. The Vietnamese are more inclined to adapt themselves to circumstances as they transpire. And while they tend to admire the Western style of charging forward, they're not inclined to adopt it. It's very important for non-Vietnamese to remain patient and relaxed when conducting business here. Many experienced business travelers feel that if 75 percent of their appointments show up, they can consider their trip a success.

Despite genuine enthusiasm for *doi moi* and foreign investment, the Vietnamese maintain a strong sense of national pride. They genuinely believe that if they had to, they could carry on without outside funds or imported expertise. And they know that if you can't provide the terms they're looking for, somebody else surely will in time. Currently, there's no shortage of foreigners looking for profitable opportunities.

While the country is truly a frontier where nearly anything goes, a certain protocol has already developed, as defined in the list that follows.

Business Guidelines for Non-Vietnamese

1. Learn about the country.

Read everything you can about Vietnam, its history and its people. Historical events and foreign domination have had a strong impact. Trying to conduct business here without some idea of the country's background will put you at a distinct disadvantage.

Identify publications and organizations pertinent to your endeavor and obtain as much information from them as possible. Meet with people who have been to Vietnam and ask about their impressions of this unusual country. Make extensive use of the Internet to research and network with experienced investors.

2. Make local contacts.

Contact as many people in Vietnam as you can before you arrive (sources for initial contacts are listed in the back of this book). Let them know what week you'll be in their vicinity and ask if you can contact them once you arrive to set up a specific appointment. And be prepared to be flexible.

3. Make a personal visit.

Your initial visit should be for research purposes; a 30-day tourist visa should suffice. Use your time to meet people (both potential business associates and the citizenry at large) and to visit government offices. Travel around the country. Get a feel for the culture and for the regional differences.

4. Find a Vietnamese partner.

Use your initial contacts to begin the search for a local partner. Many dependable foreign companies specialize in helping to arrange such matches.

5. Start with the basics.

Representative offices are no longer permitted for new companies, so it's best to find a partner who is already established in business. (And foreign firms are no longer required to open an office in Hanoi before being allowed to operate elsewhere in the country.)

Be aware that rent for foreigners is among the most expensive in Asia, and year-in-advance payments are usually required for both commercial and residential leases.

6. Obtain a license.

Joint ventures require an investment license (which will be revoked if a project isn't underway within six months of issue). In order to apply for one, you'll need a detailed feasibility study, a budget, a site proposal, construction plans, details of the joint venture contract and various other backup documentation. You and your partner should be in constant contact with the MPI, as well as the relevant central and local ministries and People's Committees.

7. Proceed slowly.

Take time to build up your business. Test the waters, and your partner, with small transactions. Under no circumstances should you forward all of your inventory or investment capital until you're firmly established. Keep in mind that you're operating in a country with little or no commercial law. Scant recourse exists for projects that go awry.

While large amounts of capital (the equivalent of hundred of millions of U.S. dollars) may give a company greater influence and leverage, some experienced investors stress the wisdom of smaller projects — arguing that Vietnam isn't yet in a position to deal effectively with huge ventures.

8. Learn the language.

The Vietnamese language is both beautiful and complex. There are more than a dozen words for "you," and each reflects the relationship between the speakers. The opportunities for misunderstanding are enormous. Although English is fast becoming the second language, you'll never really know what's going on, or be able to motivate your employees, until you master *Tieng Viet* to some extent. It's an essential skill for those serious about working in this country.

A Note on Gift Giving

In Buddhist cultures, a gift is thought to benefit the giver, rather than the recipient. If you spend a lot of time with one individual who has shown you special kindness, it's perfectly appropriate to present him or her with a substantial token of your appreciation. Appropriate gifts include picture books from your country, perfume, good whisky or cognac, expensive pens, fine chocolates and cigarettes.

Flowers are fine, but avoid chrysanthemums (used for funerals) and yellow blossoms (associated with betrayal); pink roses are for lovers. Avoid giving handkerchiefs (*khan* is associated with *kho* ("difficulty") and *kho khan* means "hardship") or anything black (a mourning color). Items that are unobtainable in Vietnam are particularly appreciated.

All gifts should be neatly wrapped, but don't expect the recipient to open it in your presence as this is considered rude. Likewise, if you receive a gift, don't open it in front of the giver. To avoid running afoul of prohibitions on bribery, develop a policy (either personal, professional or both) regarding gift giving and adhere to it.

(Also see Corporate Gifts, page 57.)

Time

Appointments

The Vietnamese have a relatively relaxed approach to time. Business is conducted late into the evening and sometimes early in the morning. Flexibility is essential.

Your Vietnamese associate will usually be prompt for appointments. However, everyone is aware of the logistical problems of travel anywhere in Vietnam, so there's no need for, or offer of, detailed explanations when someone arrives late. Should your appointment get cancelled, make every effort to reschedule. This will demonstrate your commitment to success.

If you're traveling by ground transport from one city to another, don't rely on map distances to calculate travel time. Roads are notoriously bad in the countryside, and traveling 50 kms can conceivably take hours.

Don't attempt to drive yourself anywhere until you're thoroughly familiar with the area. Most major hotels will be happy to arrange reliable transportation for you.

Agendas

Foreign businesspeople often remark that even when Vietnamese officials and business associates are punctual, they usually don't seem driven to accomplish things quickly. This can be frustrating to foreigners accustomed to conducting business at a very fast pace. But the Vietnamese will not look kindly on attempts to rush them, unless you can provide adequate reasons for quickening the pace.

Part of Vietnam's current acclimation to the world at large involves the introduction of common business practices. Experienced foreign business negotiators announce both their departure time and what they intend to accomplish at the beginning of meetings. This is especially useful when schedules are constrained by air travel. However, this method of "agenda setting" isn't recommended during the early stages of "socializing" with Vietnamese contacts.

Deadlines

The Vietnamese have a deep regard for commitments and other people's schedules. However, they've had very little experience with formal business obligations and have not yet come to see the value of written contractual terms and agreements. As in many Asian cultures, they're more likely to honor a deadline based on their personal sense of obligation to you than on a formal contract.

In addition, due to the undeveloped business infrastructure and the massive government bureaucracy, delays are inherent. Many times, these will be entirely outside the control of your Vietnamese associates. Expect the unexpected and have a contingency plan. Keep in mind that trust is at the heart of any deal in Vietnam. You must be able to meet inconveniences with smiles, rather than accusations.

12 Business Meetings

Arranging the Meeting

Due to the expense, most of your communication with Vietnam from your home country will be one-way. However, with enough persistence and a sizable phone bill, it's possible to set up a full schedule of meetings before you arrive.

(Meetings can also be arranged through the VCCI, or through service companies and consultants, who will put together an introductory study mission for you, including several meetings with interested Vietnamese, at a relatively low cost. Many foreign governments send trade missions to Vietnam; you may wish to attach yourself to one of these. The Internet is especially useful for locating these services.)

If you're communicating by fax, be very specific, both as to the content and purpose of the meeting, and the time you propose to meet. Have the fax translated into Vietnamese and double-checked for accuracy. Follow it up with a phone call, and use a translator if possible. Shortly before your arrival in Vietnam, confirm your intentions by fax (but don't expect a reply). After you arrive, call all your proposed appointments to reconfirm —

and be prepared to rearrange and reschedule your agenda. It is a good idea to arrange for an interpreter; your hotel can assist in this area.

Preparing for the Meeting

Do lots of research. Learn what the Vietnamese are looking for and what they have to offer, then tailor your proposal accordingly. There are many foreigners nosing around the country. The more information you have, the better you'll be able to distinguish your proposal from those of your competitors.

When you meet with senior officials, it's imperative that you're well prepared (a solid agenda and a specific proposal) and ready to come to at least a preliminary understanding, should the opportunity arise. The "socializing" is minimal at this level. If the Vietnamese perceive that you have nothing concrete to offer, you will probably not be invited back.

Try to obtain a photograph of the person you'll be meeting with, so that you can recognize him or her instantly. Most of the ministries publish guides to their officers. (The Vietnamese rarely smile for official photographs, so don't be put off by their grim countenances.) The Vietnamese place a high value on personal relationships. If you can't obtain a photo, ask your interpreter or another contact to describe that person to you.

Preparing the Vietnamese for the Meeting

If possible, have all written materials (including business cards) translated into Vietnamese prior to the meeting, and again, double-check them for accuracy. Mail or fax a detailed document outlining the matters to be discussed, along with a hierarchical list of the team members who'll be visiting. Include their full names, titles and genders (use Mr., Mrs. and

Miss — never Ms.), their roles on the team and photographs, if possible. Identify the team leader by putting his or her name at the top and by including more information about them than any of the others. This information will help the Vietnamese to prepare their own materials.

When scheduling meetings and negotiations, remember to allow extra time for language difficulties, a certain lack of business sophistication and the often unforeseen delays caused by an inadequate infrastructure. Carefully investigate communication options for the type of business you intend to conduct.

Whenever possible, have a reliable interpreter (of your own choosing) available. Interpreters provided by your Vietnamese counterparts will feel little loyalty for your company and its position. If you can afford to bring an interpreter from your home country, all the better. If not, your embassy or consulate may be able to secure one for you.

Kafkaesque Bureaucracy

The bureaucracy in Vietnam is rife with pitfalls and an inherent lack of urgency. Economic conditions change almost daily, as the government seeks to attain a balance between economic freedom and political control. So be forewarned.

Unless you're attempting a major infrastructure project, your negotiations will not begin "at the top." Because deals take so long to consummate and are based on personal relationships, senior officials often delegate preliminary meetings to lower level employees. In fact, they'll become involved in the process only after a relationship with their agency has been well established and they've decided that they want to work with you.

Mid-level clerks in the ministries often have

lots of "gatekeeper" decision-making authority. Your relationships with them may be the determining factor as to whether or not you ever meet the actual decisionmaker.

Business Card Protocol

Private offices are scarce in Vietnam. When you arrive for a meeting, you'll probably be escorted to a small conference room (often the only air-conditioned room available). You and your party will be seated on one side of the table and your hosts on the other. Tea or coffee will probably be served. On warmer days some companies also offer fresh coconut milk (in the shell).

Meetings open with handshakes and the exchange of business cards. It's important to shake hands and exchange cards with the most senior person present first. Cards are delivered and accepted with both hands and dutifully read as a sign of respect — don't rush to pocket or file the cards away. To keep names and faces straight, it is acceptable to spread the business cards in front of you when seated, but never write on them in front of your hosts. It will be taken as a sign of disrespect.

Telling Who's Who

The leader of the Vietnamese team will probably enter the room last or will be seated at the head of the table. It shouldn't be too difficult to spot him (it will usually be a man), as the other team members will be openly deferential.

Don't rely on titles (they're often assigned arbitrarily and don't always correspond to Western titles) or on who is doing most of the talking. Leaders often allow a subordinate to run the meeting. A reliable interpreter will be able to determine who the leader is and should be instructed (prior to the meeting) to discretely indicate who's who once the meeting begins.

Presenting Your Proposal

All business conversation is preceded by social chit-chat, which lasts much longer then many foreigners may be used to. It's best to allow your Vietnamese host to control the meeting's pace at this stage. He will most likely begin serious discussion by providing a brief history of his company or agency. Listen attentively and direct your gaze at the speaker, not the interpreter. Maintain a pleasant demeanor throughout.

Begin your segment of the meeting by thanking your hosts for their time and stating your purpose in very general, diplomatic terms. Be humble and gracious, as these traits are highly respected. After the Vietnamese respond to your proposal in general terms, you can move on to specifics.

Both before and during your visit, make the nature of your business clear. When meeting with mid-level employees, thoroughly explain the details of your project or proposal. Though the Vietnamese are new to capitalism and entrepreneurship, they're eager and fast learners. Be prepared to repeat your proposal to numerous intermediaries, and make sure your contacts understand the terminology you use. And remember that a smiling nod doesn't necessarily indicate agreement or comprehension.

Although you'll most likely be using an interpreter, your Vietnamese counterparts may start speaking your language as the meeting progresses. This is especially true of English, French, German or Russian. Your attempts to speak Vietnamese, no matter how crude, will be met with enthusiasm.

Learning a few phrases will endear you to the hosts and make them feel that you're willing to meet them halfway.

Before giving a presentation, it's imperative to have as much of your materials translated into Vietnamese as possible. Ideally, you should send a kit of materials to each individual who'll be attending the presentation. A typical kit should contain:

- A brochure describing your company
- An overview of your company that includes the names and titles of its top executives, its philosophy, values and mission statement, a list of its products and services and a short history. References to other international business endeavors should be included here.
- A short biography of the top executive and of the delegation's leader. American businessmen of a certain age bracket will always be asked if they served in the military and in Vietnam. The Vietnamese hold military service in high honor, even when confronted with former enemies. (Be advised that engaging in political discussions will not work to your advantage. Keep the past in the past.)
- Information demonstrating the success and experience of your company in providing the products or services you're proposing to offer, as well as facts that demonstrate that they're innovative and superior to similar offerings by other companies. Remember, the Vietnamese are being inundated by offers of foreign goods and services. Your association with famous brandnames (if you have them) will go far in assuring the Vietnamese that you're both reliable and reputable.

Concluding the Meeting

Allow your hosts to respond to your proposal and ask you questions. Be aware that sometimes the questions will be few or even nonexistent. This doesn't necessarily reflect a lack of interest; your counterparts may simply wish to study your proposal first. Let them know that your team is available for further discussion, and don't be surprised if a dinner invitation is forthcoming. Much of Vietnam's business is concluded over meals.

As the meeting concludes, your team leader should thank the head of the Vietnamese group personally, expressing appreciation for the opportunity to meet. Again, be gracious and humble. Thank everybody present for their time.

Each member of your team should say goodbye personally and shake hands with everybody in the room, with as much respect for rank as possible.

Corporate Gifts

In the world of Asian business, gifts are sometimes expected. Items bearing your company logo (i.e. desk calendars, lapel pins, quality pens) are often presented at the end of follow-up meetings and upon signing a deal. The Vietnamese are aware that gift giving isn't an established tradition in the West, and they will appreciate the extra care you will have taken to work within their culture.

Don't be extravagant, as this will make it difficult for the Vietnamese to reciprocate. (Nor should you be cheap, as it will reflect badly on your company.) Also, don't send the presents before the meeting; the gesture may be misinterpreted.

13 Negotiating with the Vietnamese

The Vietnamese are shrewd negotiators. Although they may be unfamiliar with many modern business methods and international finance, they're extremely pragmatic — and they know how to drive a hard bargain. They prefer to advance their position with smaller victories than to pursue one grand stroke, a philosophy best stated in the proverb: *One mouthful can be as good as the whole bowl when you're hungry.*

Always be patient, calm, polite — and persistent. Any show of frustration or anger will delay, or even end, negotiations. At the very least, such behavior will make your Vietnamese counterparts very uncomfortable. Refrain from sending representatives to a meeting who have difficulty controlling their emotions. This cannot be stressed enough. The Vietnamese are extremely measured, soft-spoken, and diligent in their approach. They associate self-control and a calm demeanor with intelligence. Act accordingly.

It's important to emphasize your long-term commitment to the country during negotiations. Stress your successes elsewhere in the international market, in Asia in particular. Focus on building a fruitful, harmonious relationship, rather than on costs or profits. If the Vietnamese sense that you're merely looking to exploit an opportunity, there's a strong chance that they'll refuse to proceed.

Vietnamese are generally practical, flexible and tend to take calculated risks. However, because they believe that knowledge is a source of both power and wealth, they'll want to gather information from a variety of sources, and discuss options and alternatives, before making business decisions.

Vietnamese Negotiating Tactics

Everything is negotiable in Vietnam, from the price of homemade medicinal ointments in the marketplace to multimillion dollar corporate ventures. So be prepared to haggle.

While you and your Vietnamese counterparts may agree on the generalities of your proposal, every point will be examined to see if additional concessions will be made. Never put your best offer up front, and never concede an issue without first making some attempt to discuss it.

However, don't bargain so vigorously that you cause your potential associates to "lose face." The Vietnamese don't approach negotiations with the objective of "winning." *"Knowing what is enough,"* they say, *"makes contentment possible."*

The following six tactics are commonly employed during negotiation sessions.

1. **Patience**

The Vietnamese are accustomed to exercising enormous patience, something they perceive Westerners as being unable to do. "Time is money" is not a Vietnamese concept, and a "take it or leave it" approach by your company won't be well received. They're patient because the current pace of their culture makes patience feasible.

Once the stakes are high enough, they'll inevitably embrace a more Western sense of "urgency," just as the "dragons" of Asia (Hong Kong, Singapore, Thailand and Taiwan) did before them. Until then, make sure that you're not locked into too tight of a schedule. It will only work against you.

2. Changing the Deal

The Vietnamese will often change an agreement's terms — overnight, and seemingly arbitrarily — even after you thought a deal had been struck, as a way of shifting the balance in their favor. Since there's little commercial law to enforce contracts, make sure that only the minimum amount of capital necessary for a project is turned over to the Vietnamese at any one time. It's not advisable to extend unsecured credit to a Vietnamese partner.

3. Playing Suitors Against Each Other

Until recently, the Vietnamese were able to play anxious suitors off against another. But an investment downswing has tipped the scales in favor of foreign capital. Vietnam is seen as being not nearly as attractive as it was two years ago, and some foreign companies have pulled out of major projects.

Let it be known that your company is willing to do business, but only in areas that show promise of investment returns within a reasonable period of time. This may be the most effective negotiation tool available to you.

4. Ambiguity

Many terms will be left unspecified by the Vietnamese, especially if they feel it's not to their advantage to clarify them. Your attempts to obtain a specific response will be continually met with vague nods or rapid changes of subject. Don't sign anything until the contract is "transparent." It's hard enough to enforce a contract in Vietnam without adding vagueness to the procedure.

5. Delays

Bureaucratic red tape is often used as an excuse for delays. Your counterparts realize that you have time constraints (due to overseas travel), and they hope that exploiting such constraints will force concessions that you wouldn't otherwise make.

The easiest way to deal with this is to play off of the competitive spirit of the Vietnamese. Make it known early on in your discussions that your company will be pursuing many other projects within the country, that your appointments are numerous and your agenda organized. Any business that can't be completed in the time allotted will be postponed indefinitely.

The Vietnamese will not want other cities, provinces or companies to woo your investment away from them. Most "delays" will evaporate when the specter of competition enters the negotiation.

6. Blaming the Interpreter

The Vietnamese will generally hire their own interpreter. In many cases, this is a necessity, as the primary decisionmaker will not be fluent in your language. If the negotiations aren't proceeding in their favor, however, the Vietnamese will often claim that most of the problems are the result of linguistic or cultural misunderstanding. Bringing your own interpreter can counter this tactic.

Ending the Negotiating Session

Like many Asian negotiators, the Vietnamese may try to drag out meetings in an attempt to wear down the opposition. Being in a small room filled with cigarette smoke, and drinking tea all morning while quibbling over minutia, can be tiring. If you don't feel that you're making headway at a reasonable pace, call for an adjournment and set a time for a follow-up meeting.

Remember, while you are expected to adhere to their cultural practices, there are limitations when your courtesy is being used against you. End the meeting politely. Try to leave the session with disputed issues left open-ended, rather than on a negative note. Chances are that one side or the other will come up with a positive alternative before the next session.

Say your good-byes to each member of the Vietnamese team directly, but always address the leader first. Don't leave any business cards lying on the table when you go.

Dealing with Interpreters

Most Vietnamese are not yet familiar with the nuances and specifics of business terms and language. If you're travelling to a number of cities or regions, you may wish to hire a different interpreter in each one, due to linguistic diversities and cost savings. The optimal situation would be to bring a trained interpreter from your home country, someone most likely to have your interests at heart. (There are close to 3 million Vietnamese living outside of their homeland.)

And keep in mind that a translator can also be invaluable when it comes to interpreting Vietnamese body language and explaining the idiosyncrasies of Vietnamese customs and behavior.

It's important to ascertain (politely but quickly) how well the translator speaks your language; many will pretend to understand, even when they don't. Work closely with your interpreter from the beginning and practice before a meeting. Negotiations will proceed much more smoothly if you've worked out some sort of system. Remember that the Vietnamese speak very softly; don't ask your interpreter to speak louder unless you really can't hear what he or she is saying.

You'll be expected to pick up your interpreter's expenses in addition to providing a salary. A "tip" at the close of each business day is not expected, but it will go a long way toward maintaining loyalty during drawn-out negotiations.

Make sure that your interpreter is well rested and prepared for each days' work. And be aware that if you hire interpreters in Vietnam, they will most likely be asked to report on your activities to local authorities. Be careful what you say in front of them, and refrain from taking them into your confidence.

Contracts, Vietnamese-style

Contract rights and obligations are not yet well understood in Vietnam, nor is there much in the way of contract law. Rapid — and sometimes arbitrary — changes take place in the economy and laws sometimes change without notice. (Sometimes they're changed and then applied retroactively to obligations already undertaken.) The Vietnamese are being advised from all quarters regarding their legal system, so the current situation is a mixture of French, Japanese, Singaporean and American jurisprudence. In addition, the cumbersome and unpredictable bureaucracy makes any contractual agreement inherently unreliable.

As a foreign businessperson, you must remain flexible and focused on your objectives. (Proceed with the idea that obtaining all of the necessary "facts" for a project will require a great deal more digging than normally needed.) Insist on compliance with an agreement's terms and conditions. Let the Vietnamese know how to maintain your continued confidence. They're innovative, industrious and accustomed to working around an inefficient system. If they trust you, they'll try hard to maintain the relationship and perform satisfactorily. Having a high-ranking government official as your ally will add to your chances of success.

Be aware that if the relationship does break down, you'll receive little in the way of protection or recourse in the Vietnamese courts. Many of the laws are new and untested. The judiciary is relatively unschooled in contractual law, and it's incapable of providing satisfaction for most breaches. If your contract was with a government agency your situation is hopeless. Vietnam's acceptance into ASEAN and eventual adherence to World Trade Organization (WTO) regulations will greatly improve this situation.

It's best to anticipate potential problem areas and to protect yourself from the beginning. (One area to consider is the eventual liquidation of a project's assets. Currently, some investors are resorting to offshore holding companies.) Local advisory offices of international law firms in both Ho Chi Minh City and Hanoi are familiar (to the extent possible) with Vietnamese business law. They can offer invaluable assistance when it comes to drafting agreements. Though foreign law firms are technically barred from practicing in areas covered by Vietnamese law, this restriction is rarely enforced.

 Business Outside the Law

The Underground Economy

Vietnam supports a huge underground economy. Experts estimate that about 45 percent of imported store merchandise (especially low-priced consumer goods) is smuggled, 35 percent is semi-official and only about 20 percent has been fully declared in terms of duties, approvals and quotas. In some cases, the smuggling is connected to local officials. Meanwhile, those trying to conduct business legally may have to wait three months to get their goods cleared at customs. Drug smuggling is dealt with severely; penalties range from long jail sentences and fines to execution.

The trade in exotic animals remains highly lucrative, despite the recent passage of stringent regulations designed to protect endangered species. "Animal acquisition centers" offer everything from live tigers and fruit bears to rare snakes and ivory. In addition, there's a regular business built around confiscating illegal goods purchased by tourists, in order to resell them to the next wave of tourists seeking to beat the system.

Foreign businesspeople must be especially careful when undertaking to buy or sell supposedly name-brand goods. They'll have very little legal protection or recourse if tricked into dealing in counterfeit goods. Although the government has begun a crackdown on counterfeit merchandise (much of it from China), bogus goods continue to flood the marketplace.

Intellectual property remains almost wholly exposed to piracy, although the government has promised to be in a position to effectively enforce these rights within the next few years. Vietnam's cities, like others worldwide, are home to a coterie of con-artists, drug dealers, motorcycle thieves, prostitutes, pursesnatchers and pickpockets.

Like many Third World countries, there's a black market for local currency. However, through several measures (including the frequent fixing of the official exchange rate of the *dong* against other major hard currencies), the government has managed to minimize its activity. Unofficial money changers boldly ply their trade directly in front of government buildings, but their rate of exchange isn't significantly different from the official rate.

Graft and Corruption

In much of developing Asia, bribery is viewed as standard protocol; it exists, to a large extent, because public servants are so poorly paid. The Vietnamese government is less than enthusiastic when it comes to responding to complaints from foreigners. Although more than one prominent Communist Party member has noted that internal corruption poses a larger threat than any perceived foreign enemy, and although some party members have recently been sentenced to prison on corruption charges, enforcement of anti-graft laws is sporadic and "show" trials often ensue.

According to the *Tuoi Tre* newspaper, the government claims to have uncovered over 17,000 economic crimes in 1995. One involved customs inspectors who had agreed to pool any bribes that exceeded US$45. When their "mutual fund" was discovered, it was accumulating US$20,000 a month.

Many foreigners pay ministry officials to obtain contracts, licenses or tax concessions. However, some claim that such tactics are never necessary, because if one official refuses to grant the approvals, there's always another door to try. In any event, corruption generally adds 10 to 15 percent to the cost of doing business.

There have been reports by arriving foreigners having to bribe Vietnamese immigration officials at the ports of entry in both Hanoi and HCMC, even when all documentation was in order. These instances are becoming fewer and fewer, but returning *Viet Kieu* remain especially hard hit.

Large signs in airport immigration and customs areas warn travelers to refrain from sliding cash into their passports and documents. If you're propositioned for (or intimidated into making) a bribe at this point, ask to see the official's superior. In most cases. the bribe request will be withdrawn.

Foreigners visiting smaller towns are often stopped (on one pretext or another, while driving or being driven), only to be released after a small cash payment. Police do set up intermittent roadblocks to stop buses and freight trucks for bribes. However, they don't pinpoint foreigners and will often wave them through, if recognized in time. If you're stopped in this way, a minimal payment will probably suffice. Or, you may be able to counteract the situation by asking for a receipt or demanding to see a superior. Your chances of arrest for refusing to pay are next to nil, unless you become abusive or violent.

U.S. Citizens and Bribery

Citizens of the United States are answerable to a special set of criteria when it comes to working within graft-ridden systems. The Foreign Corrupt Practices Act (FCPA), passed into law in the mid-1970s, makes it illegal for U.S. citizens to bribe officials of foreign countries, either directly or through an intermediary, without facing the possibility of felony charges. This puts U.S. businesspeople at a distinct disadvantage in a country like Vietnam. Not only are competitors from Europe and Asia permitted to bribe, but they can, in some cases, deduct those bribes from the taxes they pay in their countries of origin.

The FCPA does make allowances for what it calls "facilitation payments," which can be loosely described as payments to ensure that an official does what he or she was supposed to do anyway. This covers most petty bribes to police and custom officials, and even the extra charges that arise during a simple telephone installation.

U.S. investors should have a clear understanding of the FCPA before entering into serious, high-level transactions in Vietnam. (Many state up front that they have no intention of paying bribes to anyone involved in the business proposal.) Professional legal advice may be in order. The Vietnamese are aware of these restrictions, so you can expect the graft to be attached to charges for project-related goods and services.

The system will eventually improve, as it has in other developing economies. Until then, Americans are advised to protect both their legal status and their company's assets.

Two-Tier Pricing

Foreigners, regardless of their nationality, are

viewed as ready sources of cash — and the Vietnamese are relentless in their pursuit of hard currency. At the same time, Vietnam doesn't want to price its own citizens out of the market. Hence, the two-tiered pricing system evolved, and no attempt is made to hide it. Non-Vietnamese pay six to ten times more than locals. "Foreigner Prices" are posted in plain view in trains stations, restaurants, museums, hotels and the local zoo, among other places, and they even apply to internal airfares.

But travelers can take heart in the fact that even the marked-up prices are good bargains. You can haggle price, if you wish, but you'll rarely end up paying the local rate. Some expatriates who are fluent in Vietnamese pay local prices in their immediate neighborhoods, where they're known, but elsewhere they're treated like any other rich foreigners.

Present Changes and Future Outlook

The government has taken several major steps to make the Vietnamese economy more transparent, and to bring business practices into line with international standards. However, most of these efforts remain in the "directive" stage. Progress remains incremental.

The central authorities remain hampered by powerful special interests, which influence local bodies and committees. Poverty and the general inability to make ends meet are widespread. Tax evasion, believed to be rampant, is justified on the grounds that officials are corrupt. Local authorities, especially in the countryside, have no incentive to end questionable practices that net them additions to their meager incomes. It will probably be a some time before any substantive change occurs.

Names & Greetings

Name Order

The Vietnamese surname is followed by a middle name and then by a given or "first" name (as in Nguyen Minh Tuan) — a sequence designed to emphasize the primacy of the family. Some names (like Bac, which means "north") are given to children for specific reasons, and the person may insist on being called by that name, regardless of its placement in the sequence. As over half the population carries the surname Nguyen, people are commonly addressed by their given names, which are prefaced by Mr., Mrs., Miss or Madame. Until about twenty years ago, women adopted their husband's family name when they married, as in the West. This is no longer true.

Professional titles are always utilized. Therefore, a Vietnamese physician named Nguyen Minh Tuan would be addressed as Doctor (*Bac Si*) Tuan. It is also acceptable to use a professional title in conjunction with Mr. or Mrs, etc., as in Mr. Director or Mrs. Doctor. As the level of formality is relatively high, the Mr., Mrs. or Miss preface is used long after a non-Vietnamese might ordinarily have switched to using someone's first name only.

When introducing yourself, stick to the format of your home country. The Vietnamese will understand and will address you with appropriate politeness and courtesy. Generally, they'll preface your "first" name with a Mister or Miss.

Because the Vietnamese language is so sensitive to gender, marital status and age, foreigners must get used to divulging these aspects of their personal lives early in a conversation. This will enable the Vietnamese to introduce you properly in their language.

Greetings

Generally, people greet one another (and also take their leave) by shaking hands while slightly bowing their heads, with eyes averted. For very formal occasions and with very special guests, the Vietnamese give a two-handed shake, with their left hand lightly holding their right wrist. The showing of both hands is a gesture that symbolizes respect and a lack of hidden agendas.

Unlike the Japanese, the Vietnamese don't follow a rigid protocol, but there are certain acknowledged courtesies. As long as you're polite and cordial, you're unlikely to offend. The Vietnamese are used to foreign visitors and they will not take you to task for failing to follow their traditions to the letter.

Non-Vietnamese are sometimes astonished at the warm response they receive throughout the country. Initial greetings will often be accompanied by an invitation to a home or restaurant, either for a meal or a cup of rich Vietnamese coffee.

Vietnamese who know each other well address each other in terms that indicate the nature of their relationship. Those of roughly the same age will call each other *anh* (older brother) or *chi* (older sister), followed by a first name. After you know them awhile, Vietnamese acquaintances may apply one of these titles to you. Consider it a compliment. (The standard, more formal greeting is *"chao anh"* or *"chao chi,"* with *chao* meaning either hello or goodbye.)

Business Titles

Except for higher level professional designations, business titles are not particularly important or relevant in Vietnam. Most companies are structured quite loosely, and many utilize titles obtained arbitrarily through their dealings with foreigners.

It's difficult to compare company designations with common corporate titles. A "director" (*giam doc*) for instance, could mean anything from a mid-level manager to a principle on a corporate board of directors. Vice presidencies are handed out quite liberally in some organizations, but aren't used at all in others.

Keep in mind that seniority plays a major role in Vietnamese organizations and that it supersedes knowledge and skill. Younger officials rarely oversee their elders, regardless of the quality of their technical or managerial skills.

Exchanging Business Cards

At meetings, hand shakes precede the handing out of cards. (Occasionally, a woman may not extend her hand. If this happens, respond with a slight bow of the head and a smile.)

Vietnamese are almost as fanatical about business cards as the Japanese, although they exchange them with a great deal less ceremony. Be sure to carry a good supply with you at all times.

While it's not very difficult to have business

cards made in Vietnam, it's best to bring them from your home country, especially if you wish to repli-cate a company logo. It's a nice gesture to have one side printed in Vietnamese, if possible. (Make sure to double-check the translation.)

Vietnamese business cards are very simple; and high government officials often have little more than their name on them. This is because most government officials carry two types of cards. One, containing all needed contact information, is used for formal meetings, when future contact is desirable. Plain name cards are used for informal or unofficial meetings. Many ministers carry the latter when they're overseas, to prevent people from reading more into a meeting than necessary. If you receive one of these plain cards, don't take it as an insult or press for further contact information. The person that gave it to you is working within the restrictions of his or her bureaucracy.

Use discretion when handing out your own business cards. Keep in mind that anyone you give one to will consider the gesture significant; they may even use your card as a reference. And that "reference" may come back to haunt you. Vietnam is a country where networking and name dropping rule the day. A casual but unscrupulous acquain-tance may use your card as an introduction to another business deal.

Communication Styles

Politeness At All Costs

In keeping with Confucian values of harmony, the Vietnamese are soft spoken, courteous and invariably polite. Rarely will you hear a voice raised even to beckon somebody above the noise and commotion of the city. Though they make eye contact while talking, they tend to keep it to a minimum.

Aggressive come-ons and fast-talking sales pitches (commonplace among some Western businesspeople) will only serve to make the Vietnamese uncomfortable and jeopardize the success of your proposal, regardless of its merits.

Many Vietnamese are not yet familiar with Western business terminologies and will be inclined to nod in agreement, pretending to understand when they do not. And some terms simply don't translate well. Be thorough with both your interpreter and your Vietnamese hosts. Avoid misunderstandings by carefully discussing and explaining the specifics of your transactions.

Nonverbal Communication

Broad hand and arm motions to elaborate a

point. Slouching in a chair when tired. Briefly touching an acquaintance on the arm or shoulder while talking. These are common gestures in many societies, but the Vietnamese find them troublesome. These actions are simply not consistent with the subdued, polite interchanges with which they're familiar. It's in your best interest to refrain from using them.

The Intricacies of a Smile

A smile generally indicates pleasure and a welcoming attitude. But be aware that it can also indicate irritation, dismay or even ignorance of the subject at hand.

If controversial topics or possible areas of confrontation arise, the Vietnamese will usually attempt to cover their discomfort with a smile. Don't take this to mean that they agree with your statements. They 're merely putting a pleasant face on a situation they find uncomfortable.

The Vietnamese realize that they're at a great disadvantage when it comes to investment capital, technology and business acumen. Whereas some cultures might cover their ignorance with arrogance or belligerence, the Vietnamese use a smile as a way to save face, while, at the same time, encouraging continued dialogue.

Anger is considered a loss of self-control and, once again, the smile is used to cover true feelings. Thus, harmony is maintained and the relationship is preserved.

Guidelines for Non-Vietnamese

The following will help you to become more conscious of your body language and the ways in which it may be interpreted.

1.   Avoid Physical Contact

The Vietnamese aren't comfortable being touched, however casually, by relative strangers. Although you'll often see women holding hands and men walking arm in arm, these are old and dear friends.

2.   Keep Your Distance

In formal situations keep your distance during conversations. Westerners should keep in mind that they're generally taller than the Vietnamese, and so can appear to be physically threatening. The closer you stand together, the more the height differential is emphasized.

All proximity rules are suspended, however, in crowded buses or public areas, where physical contact is tolerated but the individuals involved withdraw by averting their eyes and avoiding interaction.

3.   Do As They Do

Follow the lead of your hosts. The Vietnamese don't maintain rigid rules of social interaction, but they always err in favor of courtesy. Some people are friendlier than others, of course, and the South tends to be more relaxed than the North.

4.   Speak Softly

Always maintain a calm demeanor. Never ever raise your voice (especially in anger) or speak louder than is necessary to be heard. This is a sure sign that you lack self-control and are, therefore, unreliable.

5.   Keeps Your Hands Down

The Vietnamese don't gesture much when they speak, and they will not understand your gestures. It's best to refrain from emphasizing your points with excessive hand movements.

6.   Listen More - Talk Less

Listen carefully, wait for others to finish, and don't talk too much. The Vietnamese will rarely interrupt another's conversation, and they find that Europeans and Americans are often extremely rude in this regard.

7. Posture Matters

Balance is highly valued principle in all aspects of Vietnamese life. Slouching and other "inharmonious" postures aren't looked on favorably. Even the poorest bicycle riders on a crowded street, regardless of age, sit ramrod straight, carrying themselves with great dignity.

8. Remember Your Status

Foreigners (especially those from the more assertive Western cultures) should allow their Vietnamese hosts to take the lead. Don't patronize or condescend. Your manners, more than your investment offer, will determine whether or not you're invited to return.

9. Don't Point

Never point at another person. In fact, it's a good idea to avoid pointing altogether. If you need to indicate something, do so with your whole hand, with the palm opened upward.

Customs

The Influence of Buddhism

Vietnam is primarily a Buddhist country. (There's a sizable population of Catholics in the South, and Hanoi even boasts a cathedral.) Every major city has one or more Buddhist temples, and virtually every home and shop displays a small ancestor shrine with offerings of food and incense. It's believed that souls need tending so that they can watch over living family members, and possibly even protect them by way of warning dreams. Neglected souls become lonely and wander aimlessly.

Cao Daism (a religion that developed in the 1920s and combines Buddhism, Christianity and Taoism) is an example of how Vietnam absorbs outside influences and synthesizes them into something uniquely its own. Its approximately two million followers recognize saints ranging from Buddha and Christ to Joan of Arc, Napoleon Bonaparte and novelist Victor Hugo.

Tet: the Lunar New Year

Most Vietnamese save up their money all year for this national equinox festival. The date varies, depending on the Lunar Calendar, but it's generally celebrated around February (*Thang Hai*) and lasts anywhere from three days to two weeks.

Offices, farm production and government agencies all grind to a virtual halt as the country prepares. (Business travelers are advised to plan accordingly.) Old debts are settled, houses are cleaned and new clothes are bought. It's estimated that as many as 40,000 *Viet Kieu* return to Vietnam each year to enjoy the fun (and bolster the economy with the equivalent of millions of U.S. dollars in cash and gifts). Hotel rooms and airline bookings are in short supply for up to a month during the *Tet* season, and travel visas must be applied for weeks in advance.

Homes are decorated with fresh flowers, which are changed daily, if possible. Offerings of food, cigarettes, alcohol, incense and imitation money (the bills are burned) are made to ancestors. It's a time for family gatherings and gift giving — tea, kumquat trees, candied ginger or coconut, and flowering peach or apricot branches are all believed to bring good fortune. White items (including wrapping paper and bows) are avoided. Children receive "lucky money" (*li xi*) in red envelopes.

Everything centers around food. *Banh chung* (rice cakes filled with pork and mung beans, which are wrapped in banana leaves and steamed) are a particular *Tet* treat. Every household buys a pair of watermelons; the redder the fruit, the luckier the family will be in the coming year. Be prepared to dine endlessly and richly, as the Vietnamese like to show their generosity and culture to foreigners.

Spending is so extravagant during *Tet* that the government institutes temporary price controls in order to curb inflated pricing. Until a few years ago, firecrackers played a major role in *Tet*, but they've since been outlawed. Aside from the explosion-related injuries and deaths every year, it was felt that the money spent (over US$1 million annually) could be put to better use in this poor country.

Birds, Buffaloes and Water Puppets

Some villages and provinces celebrate their own unique festivals. These include wrestling matches, rice-cooking and bird-singing contests, horse and elephant races, and firecracker and snake-catching competitions. During the Lim Festival in Ha Bac province, young boys and girls answer questions about love and courtship with impromptu singing. The Southern highland has a traditional buffalo-killing festival, and in Tay Ninh, there's an annual month-long pilgrimage to Black Lady Mountain. For *Doan Ngu* (Summer Solstice Day), offerings are made to the god of the dead in the hope of warding off disease, and human effigies are burned to satisfy his requirement for souls for his army.

Hat Boi ("songs with fancy dress") has its origins in Chinese theatre, but, like the religious festivals, is being touted as distinctly Vietnamese. The same is true of *Roi Nuoc*, the internationally renowned Water Puppets. *Hat Cheo* (popular theatre) embraces more topical and controversial themes.

 Dress & Appearance

The Vietnamese admire neatness and cleanliness. They find it difficult to understand how some tourists can dress so poorly and untidily when they have so much money. Those who dress well are accorded more respect, are assumed to be better educated, and face fewer logistical difficulties than those who don't.

Traditional Attire

Male traditional attire consists of a long-sleeved silk tunic topped with a high "mandarin" collar. Its color and embroidered symbols were determined by the wearer's rank and class. Today, these are worn only for formal occasions, such as weddings and holidays. Women, however, often wear *ao dai* (high-collared, long silk tunics, with tight-fitting bodices, that are slit up the sides to the waist and worn over pants). Pure white *ao dai* are worn by teenage schoolgirls. (Up until the early 20th century, teenage upperclass girls were still having their teeth permanently blackened with lacquer.) "Mao suits" remain popular with Communist Party members and government officials.

Conical straw hats (*non la*), almost considered a symbol of the nation, are worn by both city and farm dwellers. A formal headdress for ceremonial occasions is made by winding silken plaits into a disk shape (it's worn cocked on the back of the head). In the north, many laborers sport green army pith helmets.

The poor tend to wear whatever is available; to Western eyes, their clothing resembles pajamas. Their sandals are often handmade, though plastic versions seem to dominate, especially in the cities.

Dressing for Business

For both men and women, extravagant displays of wealth (designer suits, expensive shoes, excessive jewelry) aren't recommended. The Vietnamese don't like ostentation.

Foreign businessmen in Hanoi, Haiphong and HCMC generally wear suits and ties The hotter weather down south requires the use of air conditioning almost year-round. Once a regular business relationship has been attained, a more relaxed (i.e. open collar shirts) style can be adopted. In both regions and for both sexes, suits are appropriate attire for meeting with government officials.

Foreign businesswomen commonly wear lightweight dresses or blouses with tailored trousers or skirts. Short skirts or tight fitting clothing should be avoided, both for business and when visiting temples or shrines. (An attendant will never tell a foreigner that he or she is dressed too casually, but he may say that the shrine is "temporarily closed.")

Most hotels, even small ones, will arrange for your laundry to be done at very reasonable rates. Bring sufficient changes of clothing; it's difficult to find "off the rack" replacements, especially in larger sizes.

Reading the Vietnamese

Style and Substance

The Vietnamese are masters of innuendo and have many ways of expressing themselves without uttering a word. They can smile in a hundred different ways, not all of which connote amusement or pleasure. If, in your misunderstanding, you laugh, it will embarrass them greatly and might hurt their feelings as well.

Vietnamese will often stop making direct eye contact when they're displeased or disagree with what you're saying. While you should not address this directly, be aware of it and be prepared to change your tact, if you want the conversation to continue smoothly.

As has been previously noted, the Vietnamese are always polite and courteous. Non-Vietnamese need to be sensitive to subtle clues in order to understand what's really being conveyed.

Nonverbal Do's and Don'ts

- Never point at anyone or beckon to them by extending your arm and bending your index finger. If you can't communicate in any other way, look at the person in question and then place your open hand, palm first, against your chest.

- Never whistle to get someone's attention.
- Always use both hands to pass things from one person to the next.
- Regardless of whether or not you're wearing shoes, never expose the soles of your feet when crossing your legs or sitting on the floor. It's considered rude and disrespectful.
- Don't be surprised if your business associate tries to hold your hand while walking. This is common behavior, even between people of the same sex. It means only that he or she feels very comfortable with you.
- Never attempt to maintain eye contact with a Vietnamese who wishes to avoid it. They probably disagree with what you're saying and want to avoid confrontation.

20 Entertaining

Exotic Fare

Luckily for foreigners, the Vietnamese love to entertain over meals. This provides an excellent way to learn something about Vietnamese culture and accomplish some business at the same time.

Be prepared to be offered such dishes as sea cucumber, bat meat, sauteed grubs, stir-fried baby birds, turtle, snake, dog, or newborn chicken served in a soup. (Buddhism promotes vegetarianism but doesn't demand it.) Less exotic dishes are also to be found. Your Vietnamese hosts will probably make a great effort to feed you the "best" the country has to offer. Try not to be squeamish. Local fruits include guavas, longans, bananas, mangoes, jackfruit, green papaya and coconuts. Durian (a spiny fruit with custardy yellow flesh that's been described as "tasting like heaven but smelling like hell") is a particular favorite.

The Vietnamese will appreciate it if you try any or all of these special delicacies; but if you don't, no one will be surprised or offended. In any event, be appreciative and polite, and be sure to thank your hosts for providing you with such an interesting opportunity.

Like their Chinese neighbors, Vietnamese chefs try to balance of salty, sweet, sour, bitter and hot tastes into a pleasing meal, and vegetables play a central role. The French influence can be seen in sauce preparation, use of pâtés, coffee preferences and the ubiquitous *banh mi* baguette. As is true in most of Asia, rice is a staple. The Vietnamese word for steamed rice (*com*) is the same word for "meal."

Pho & Bun Cha — National Dishes

Pho, a noodle soup that originated in the north, is generally eaten for breakfast (with both chopsticks and a spoon) but is served throughout the day. It comes in beef, chicken and seafood styles. In the south, it's accompanied by a side dish of bean sprouts, chiles, slices of lime and hot sauces, to be added according to one's taste.

Bun cha, another northern specialty, features green vegetables (lettuce, basil, mint, cilantro and lemony *diep ca*), thick white noodles and bits of charcoal-grilled pork in a golden broth.

Dining in a Private Home

Your Vietnamese acquaintances will readily invite you into their homes. (Shoes are always removed before entering. Your host will usually provide you with sandals for indoor use.) Don't arrive early if invited for a meal. The Vietnamese often prepare complex dishes, always from the freshest ingredients, and they like everything to be perfect. (Ice coolers and small gas burners are standard; refrigerators and stoves are for the rich.) Don't bring food items or dessert, as this may be looked on as an insult to the hostess.

Communal serving dishes, from which everybody helps himself, are common. Your hosts will probably serve you first, to ensure that you receive the largest portions of everything. Take it upon yourself to make certain that there's plenty for everyone else.

Mealtime includes conversation, but the Vietnamese prefer to keep the topics light. Always make a point of complimenting the food. If you have after-dinner plans, let the host know before the meal begins.

If you try to reciprocate your host's hospitality by offering a restaurant meal, the Vietnamese may think that you're trying to out-do them. A gift to the family may be more appropriate.

Don't decide to pay a visit to a home if you haven't been invited, especially near mealtime. Having a foreign guest in one's home is considered an honor, and most Vietnamese are not in a position to entertain as they would like to, unless they can plan well in advance. At the same time, it would be unthinkable for a Vietnamese family to not invite you to join them for their meal. But they'll be uncomfortable and feel that they can't entertained you adequately. You will not be able to assure them otherwise.

In a Restaurant

Vietnamese businesspeople love to entertain in restaurants (as well as in small coffee houses, over tea, on a tour, while running errands and at social gatherings of all sorts). Although business may not seem to be the focus of conversation, many important decisions are reached in informal settings.

As with all Vietnamese meals, restaurant dining can last for hours and consist of numerous courses. Pace yourself accordingly. Your hosts will probably go to great lengths to entertain you lavishly (they'll be paying the "local" price). Never offer to pay for such a meal. Instead, reciprocate by inviting your host to partake in an equally fine meal at another time. Many of the country's best restaurants are prohibitively expensive for locals. Most businesspeople will greatly appreciate being treated to such a meal. But don't flaunt your wealth or try to outdo your host's efforts.

(Give the restaurant you've chosen a budget <u>after</u> reviewing their menu choices. Tell them how many people will be in attendance and how long you'd like the party to last. Seeking the advice of an experienced ex-patriate will save you lots of headaches.)

Smoking — A National Pastime

Male visitors will be offered cigarettes at every possible opportunity. If you smoke, make a point to offer cigarettes to others by putting your open pack on the table with a few cigarettes pulled halfway out. American-made brands are especially well received. Cigarettes are sometimes even offered as tips to *cyclo* drivers.

If you don't smoke, avoid showing signs of displeasure and don't ask the Vietnamese to refrain from smoking in your presence. If you're allergic to the smoke or simply find it noxious, find a way to control your reaction. (The government's low level anti-smoking campaign is widely ignored.)

Foreign women smokers may find themselves attracting more attention from local men than they'd like, unless they're with male companions.

Socializing

Conversation

The Vietnamese are first-class conversationalists, and they're starved for information about the rest of the world. They usually begin by asking about a guest's marital status, age and number of children. In part, this allows them to know how to properly address you. It's also true that Vietnamese view family life as the center of culture. Producing photographs of your spouse and children (or even of nieces and nephews) will be well received.

Hundreds of hastily constructed eateries and coffee shops serve as informal social salons in every city. Be cautious, however, about raising overtly political issues. Also, be aware that the central government monitors foreigners in hotels, offices, on the telephone and even in restaurants. Keep your conversations light and general, until you have a good idea to whom you're speaking.

Younger Vietnamese enjoy listening to contemporary music. Vietnamese rock bands do exist (with names like Da Vang or "Yellow Skin"), but their songs are highly regulated by the government.

Drink Protocol

Whether in a private home or in a restaurant, men will be offered large quantities of whisky and beer, often before a meal. Often, entire evenings are spent drinking, smoking cigarettes and trading stories about how business is done in other countries. This camaraderie isn't entirely social, however, so keep your wits about you. The Vietnamese are both evaluating your character and trying to obtain information and concessions.

As with cigarettes, the public consumption of alcohol by women is associated with prostitution. Women will be offered soft drinks or water (though a few more outgoing Vietnamese females may sip a glass of wine, if it's available). Foreign women who ignore this cultural taboo during business meals will reduce their chances of being taken seriously.

The importance of this pastime and the amount of business that can be conducted in this way shouldn't be underestimated. Therefore, it's advisable for a traveling businesswoman to bring along a trusted male counterpart who can socialize on her behalf.

Toasting is common. One favorite is *"Tram phan tram"* (One hundred percent!); if you hear this, you're supposedly required to empty your glass in one swallow. Take note: Vietnamese and Cambodian whiskys are less potent (and much more affordable) than their Western counterparts. But Vietnamese beer (so popular that most towns boast a local brand) has a higher alcohol content than foreign brews.

Would You Like a Companion?

Foreign businessmen are often approached by prostitutes — on the street, in bars, or even while taking a leisurely *cyclo* tour of a city (with the female in question passing by on a motorbike).

And it's not unusual, during an evening's entertainment, for a host to ask a male visitor if he'd like a "companion." This may occur even shortly after the visitor has shared dinner with the host and his wife. However, the Vietnamese understand that the Western concept of marital fidelity is often stricter than their own. Married men who decline such an invitation are shown no disrespect. Unmarried men who decline are generally assumed to be homosexual and will sometimes be offered a male companion as an option. Regardless of your views on this, be forewarned that the government takes a dim view of such activities.

Roadtrips

The Vietnamese are proud of their country and eager to share its spectacular scenery. Foreigners will sometimes be invited on sightseeing tours by their hosts; such offers should be accepted as compliments, as they're not extended casually.

It may be a trip to a local landmark or pagoda, there may be no particular destination, or your host may wish to show you his ancestral village. (Many government and business officials have family roots in the countryside.)

Besides cementing your business relationship, you'll have an opportunity to see one of the most beautiful countries in the world. Sit back and enjoy the hospitality.

CHAO ANH

 Basic Vietnamese Phrases

English	Vietnamese (no diacritics)
Yes No	*Vang* *Khong*

Hello
Hello (to men) same age /
   older
Hello (to women) same
   age /older
How are you?
	Chao
	Chao anh / Chao Ong
	
	Chao chi / Chao Ba
	
	Co Khoe khong?

Good-bye	*Tam Biet*
Please	*Xin*
Thank you	*Cam on*
Pleased to meet you	*Han hanh duoc gap.*
Excuse me; I'm sorry	*xin loi*
My name is _____	*Toi ten la _____*
What is your name?	*Ten (anh/chi/ong/ba) la gi?*
I do n't understand	*Toi khong hieu*

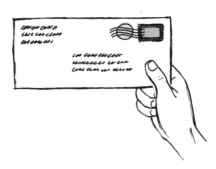

 Correspondence

In general, Vietnamese mailing addresses follow the model below:

Mr. Nguyen Son
49 Nam Ky Khoi Nghia Street
Hanoi, Vietnam

As not all packages and bulky letters reach their destinations, many businesses have their mail couriered in and out of the country.

Ho Chi Minh City is divided into *quan* (districts), and the district number is written either at the end of the second line or at the beginning of the third line, before the city name. Street addresses often are subdivided:

Mr. Phan Chin
171 / 21 Vo Thi Sau, District 3
Ho Chi Minh City, Vietnam
or
District 3, Ho Chi Minh City, Vietnam

Useful Numbers

International calls can be made from major hotels or post offices. Callers are billed from the moment the phone starts ringing. For domestic long-distance calls, dial 01, the area code and then the number. Most telephone operators understand basic English.

- Vietnam country code .... [84]
- City codes: HCMC [8]; Hanoi [4]; Danang [51]
- For international access code assistance, dial [12] or [13]
- Ministry of Commerce and Tourism (4)8257078
- Vietcochamber .... (4) 8252961
- MPI Hanoi .... (4) 8253666
- MPI Ho Chi Minh City .... (8) 8894674
- VCCI Hanoi .... (4)8253023
- VCCI HCMC .... (8)8230301
- Ministry of Culture and Information (4) 8264287
- INVESTIP .... (4) 8266185
- Saigontourist .... (8) 8230103
- Vietnam Tourism .... (4)8264319
- Vietnam Airlines .... (4) 8253842
- AEA International Hospital Hanoi (4) 8213555
- AEA International Hospital HCMC (8)8298520
- Hanoi Police .... (4) 8253131

 ## Books & Internet Addresses

Culture Shock! Vietnam by Ellis Claire. Graphic Arts Center Publishing Company, Portland, Oregon,U.S., 1995. An up-to-date, practical information source about living and doing business in Vietnam.

Doing Business in Vietnam. Chamber of Commerce and Industry of Vietnam, Hanoi, 1996. Business from the Vietnamese perspective.

Vietnam: Business Opportunities and Risks by Joseph P. Quinlan. Pacific View Press, Berkeley, California,U.S., 1995.

Vietnam's Dilemmas and Options. Institute of Southeastern Asian Studies, ASEAN Economic Research Unit, Singapore, 1993.

Internet Addresses

http://www.vietconnection.com
http://www.saigonnet.com